THE FASCINATING
SCIENCE
BOOK
FOR KIDS

THE FASCINATING
SCIENCE
BOOK
FOR KIDS

500
AMAZING
FACTS!

KEVIN KURTZ, MA

ROCKRIDGE
PRESS

Interior and Cover Designer: Linda Snorina
Art Producer: Samantha Ulban
Editor: Mary Colgan
Production Editor: Jenna Dutton

Photography & Illustrations © NASA Goddard, Neil Bromhall/ Shutterstock, Martin Valigursky/Shutterstock, Ivan Cholakov / Alamy Stock Photo, LorraineHudgins/Shutterstock, Zebra-Studio/Shutterstock, italianestro/ Shutterstock, orin/Shutterstock, Cover; NASA, p.3; Danté Fenolio/ Science Source, p.10; Visual&Written SL / Alamy Stock Photo, p.1; blickwinkel / Alamy Stock Photo, Andy Newman's Tarantulas / Alamy Stock Photo, p.20; blickwinkel / Alamy Stock Photo, p.21; Sean Prior / Alamy Stock Photo, p.23; Ridvan Arda / Alamy Stock Photo, p.25; The Protected Art Archive / Alamy Stock Photo, p.27; Daniel Eskridge / Alamy Stock Photo, p.29; sciencephotos / Alamy Stock Photo, p.32; Paulo Oliveira / Alamy Stock Photo, p.39; massimiliano finzi / Alamy Stock Photo, p.44; PRILL Mediendesign / Alamy Stock Photo, p.45; John Cancalosi / Alamy Stock Photo, p.46; Mopic / Alamy Stock Photo, p.52; World History Archive / Alamy Stock Photo, NASA/JPL-Caltech, p.53;mark Turner / Alamy Stock Photo, Torontonian / Alamy Stock Photo, p.55; Matteo Omied / Alamy Stock Photo, p.56; MasPix / Alamy Stock Photo, p.59; FLPA / Alamy Stock Photo; Albatross / Alamy Stock Photo, p.60; Nature Picture Library / Alamy Stock Photo, Riccardo Oggioni / Alamy Stock Photo, Brad Leue / Alamy Stock Photo, p.61; Photo 12 / Alamy Stock Photo, p.65; Images & Stories / Alamy Stock Photo, p.66; Peter Hermes Furian / Alamy Stock Photo, p.72; Michael Schmeling / Alamy Stock Photo, p.73; Dennis Hallinan / Alamy Stock Photo, p.75; Ivan Vdovin / Alamy Stock Photo, p.78; NASA/JPL-Caltech, p.85; SwRI/Simone Marchi, p.91; James / Alamy Stock Photo, p.94; NASA/ESA/ATG Medialab, p.97; Paul Mariess / Alamy Stock Photo,Andrey Nekrasov / Alamy Stock Photo, p.103; J. Whatmore/ The European Science Agency, p.107; World History Archive / Alamy Stock Photo, New Zealand American Submarine Ring of Fire 2007 Exploration, NOAA Vents Program, the Institute of Geological & Nuclear Sciences and NOAA-OE / Science Source, p.108; NOAA Okeanos Explorer Program, Galapagos Rift Expedition 2011 / Science Source, B. Murton/Southampton Oceanography Centre/ Science Source, p.109; Jaime Chirinos/ Science Source, p.116;frans lemmens / Alamy Stock Photo, p.117; MasPix / Alamy Stock Photo, p.118; nobeastsofierce Science / Alamy Stock Photo, p.132; Jose Antonio Penas/ Science Source, p.144; dpa picture alliance / Alamy Stock Photo, blickwinkel / Alamy Stock Photo, p.145; Koch Valérie / Alamy Stock Photo, p.147; Mopic / Alamy Stock Photo, p.148;Dmitry Larichev / Alamy Stock Photo, Łukasz Szczepanski / Alamy Stock Photo, p.149; directphoto.bz / Alamy Stock Photo, Brian Parker / Alamy Stock Photo, p.151; Stuart Clarke / Alamy Stock Photo, p.160; blickwinkel / Alamy Stock Photo, p.161; World History Archive / Alamy Stock Photo, p.164; NatPar Collection / Alamy Stock Photo, p.165; Christina Darkin/ Science Source, Nature Photographers Ltd / Alamy Stock Photo, p.170; Stan Zack / Alamy Stock Photo, p.172; Horizon International Images Limited / Alamy Stock Photo, AB Forces News Collection / Alamy Stock Photo, p.173; Turtle Rock Scientific/ Science Source, p.189; Paul Fleet / Alamy Stock Photo, p.190; Leonello Calvetti/ Science Source, p.192; Universal Images Group North America LLC / DeAgostini / Alamy Stock Photo, p.195; Neil Bowman / Alamy Stock Photo, p.197; hakan çorbacı / Alamy Stock Vector, p.201. All other images used under license Shutterstock and iStock. Author photo courtesy of Linda Saxton.

ISBN: Print 978-1-64739-870-5 | eBook 978-1-64739-547-6
R0

TO
MY EAGLE
FRIENDS

Meet Earth's sister planet, Venus!
page 106

CONTENTS

Our Marvelous Moon . . 2

Hunters with Wings . . . 4

Supervolcanoes 6

Oxygen Is Awesome . . . 8

Let It Glow! 10

Mysterious
Black Holes 12

Cool Copper 14

The Big Chill 16

Gigantic Jupiter 18

Web Spinners 20

Earth's Magnetic
Personality 22

The Human Machine . . 24

Marvelous
Mountains 26

Amazing Animals
of the Cenozoic 28

SUNsational! 30

H_2-Oh! 32

It's Shocking! 34

Meet the Dolphins 36

It's in the Blood! 38

Small, But Mighty!..... 40

The Other
Blue Planet 42

Into the Deep 44

Volcanic Rocks 46

Flower Friends....... 48

It's Invisible! 50

Colorful
Space Clouds 52

Amazing Animals
of the Cretaceous..... 54

Glittering Gold 56

When Earth Shakes... 58

Freaky Frogs......... 60

The Atmosphere
Around Us 62

Meteoroids, Meteors,
and Meteorites 64

Just Jellyfish 66

Phenomenal Fire...... 68

Zap! 70

Walls of Water 72

The Red Planet 74

Tree-mendous Trees .. 76

What color is snow?
page 140

CONTENTS

Goodbye, Dinosaurs . . . 78

Take Your Vitamins! . . . 80

Sedimentary Rocks . . . 82

The Magnificent
Milky Way 84

On the Hunt 86

Listen Up! 88

Journey to the
Center of the Earth . . . 90

Iron, Man! 92

Crafty Camouflage
and Mimicry 94

Cool Comets 96

Hot, Hot, HOT! 98

Rivers of Ice 100

Plenty of Plankton 102

Nifty Nitrogen 104

Blazing-Hot Venus 106

Ocean Chimneys 108

Backyard Science 110

**When did this predator
with five eyes live?**
page 194

Hot Spots 112

Gravity Is Groovy 114

Strange Senses 116

Seeing Stars 118

Hello, Helium! 120

Natural Partners 122

Seasons Change 124

The Ringed Planet 126

Building Blocks 128

Shifting Plates 130

Very Strange
Viruses 132

Wild Wetlands 134

Metamorphic Rocks . . . 136

When a Star Dies 138

The Sky Is Falling! 140

Incredible Infrared 142

Amazing Animals
of the Jurassic 144

Below the Surface 146

Rocks in Space 148

How thick is sea lettuce?
page 167

Something Fishy 150

Plasma Aplenty 152

Burning the Past 154

Opposites Attract 156

Mini Mercury 158

Adaptable Animals . . . 160

Cool Carbon 162

Trench Volcanoes 164

Photosynthesis
Powerhouses 166

Sun-Powered
Solar Weather 168

Spineless Wonders 170

Extreme Storms! 172

Two Sensational
Senses 174

Hot Water 176

Funky Fungi 178

Let There Be Light! 180

The Coldest Planet 182

What metal was this royal mirror made of?
page 189

Water World 184

Microscopic
Microbes 186

So Many Metals 188

Brilliant Brains 190

Earth's Crust 192

Amazing Animals
of the Paleozoic Sea . . . 194

Potent Poisons 196

Incredible Insects 198

What Don't
We Know? 200

On which planet does it rain diamonds?
page 43

How tall were terror birds?
page 29

OUR MARVELOUS MOON

Earth's moon is a **NATURAL SATELLITE** that orbits around our planet about once every 27 days.

The Moon is one-quarter the size of Earth.

A small planet smashed into Earth billions of years ago, blasting magma, rock, and dust into orbit—which eventually became the Moon.

THE LARGE, DARK SPOTS ON THE MOON ARE CALLED "SEAS," BUT THEY ARE ACTUALLY LAVA ROCK FROM ANCIENT VOLCANIC ERUPTIONS.

The Moon's largest crater, the **SOUTH POLE-AITKEN BASIN**, is 1,550 miles (2,500 km) wide and 5 miles (8 km) deep!

IF YOU COULD DRIVE to the Moon, it would take about 166 days to get there at highway speeds.

The Moon moves about 1.5 inches (3.8 cm) farther away from Earth every year.

HUNTERS
WITH WINGS

BIRDS OF PREY kill and eat other birds and small animals.

A **BALD EAGLE** may dive-bomb an osprey that just caught a fish to steal its meal.

PEREGRINE FALCONS are more closely related to parrots than they are to hawks and eagles.

A GREAT HORNED OWL is one of the only animals that will eat a skunk.

HARRIS HAWKS live in deserts with few tall plants to roost on, so they stack on top of each other when they find a perch.

KESTRELS can see the ultraviolet light reflected off some rodents' pee trails, and they use it to hunt them down.

TURKEY VULTURES have an average wingspan of 6 feet (1.8 m) but weigh less than 5 pounds (2 kg).

SUPER-VOLCANOES

A **SUPERVOLCANO** is any volcano that has erupted more than 240 cubic miles (1,000 cubic km) of lava, pumice, and ash.

YELLOWSTONE NATIONAL PARK is home to one of 20 supervolcanoes on Earth.

From space, you can see how the Yellowstone supervolcano's eruptions have moved over millions of years.

The **SIBERIAN TRAPS** supervolcano that erupted 250 million years ago caused the extinction of 90 percent of Earth's species, including trilobites like the one that left this fossil.

When India's **DECCAN TRAPS SUPERVOLCANO** erupted 66 million years ago, it covered 200,000 square miles (about 500,000 km) of land with lava more than 1 mile (1.6 km) deep.

OXYGEN
IS AWESOME

Oxygen is a **GAS** that makes up 21 percent of Earth's atmosphere.

MORE THAN HALF of the oxygen we breathe is made by seaweed and plant plankton in the ocean.

Oxygen becomes a BLUE LIQUID when it is chilled below -270°F (-168°C).

Almost half the weight of EARTH'S CRUST (outer layer) comes from oxygen.

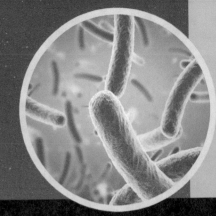

Some species of **MICROBES** are poisoned by oxygen and breathe things like iron instead.

NORTHERN LIGHTS appear green when high-energy electrons crash into oxygen atoms in the atmosphere, causing them to glow.

9

LET IT GLOW!

BIOLUMINESCENCE is the ability of animals and other living things to produce light.

Instead of using their flashing lights to attract mates, female *Photuris versicolor* FIREFLIES mimic other species' light patterns to attract males—that they eat!

Most ocean animals can't see red light, but LOOSEJAW DRAGONFISH can. They use red bioluminescence to find prey without being seen by predators.

ANGLERFISH use lures that are filled with glowing bioluminescent bacteria to attract prey.

Glowing **BIOLUMINESCENT MUSHROOMS** attract bugs that pick up their spores and drop them elsewhere to grow more mushrooms.

HUMBOLDT SQUID can both glow and change their colors to communicate while hunting in groups.

Some tiny **PLANKTON** called *dinoflagellates* produce light when they are disturbed and make ocean waves glow blue.

MYSTERIOUS BLACK HOLES

Black holes are areas of space where **GRAVITY** is so strong that not even light can escape.

There may be as many as one billion black holes in the **MILKY WAY GALAXY**.

The **LARGEST BLACK HOLE** we know about is 6.4 billion times bigger than the Sun.

There are so many black holes in the universe that there is a black-hole collision about once every five minutes.

A supermassive black hole's extreme gravity is strong enough to rip a nearby star apart and cause the star's gas to swirl around the black hole like water going down a drain.

COOL COPPER

Copper is a **PINKISH-ORANGE METAL** that is common on Earth's surface.

COPPER and **GOLD** are the only metallic elements that are not silver in color.

People need to eat small amounts of copper to make blood cells, bone, and other tissues. Copper is found in foods like nuts, leafy greens, and **DARK CHOCOLATE**.

Copper is a natural bacteria killer, so many public buildings have copper door handles to stop the spread of germs.

HORSESHOE CRABS have blueish-green blood because it contains a lot of copper.

The **STATUE OF LIBERTY** is green because it's covered in copper. Over time, copper reacts with oxygen in water and air and turns this color.

THE BIG CHILL

ICE AGES are periods of time when Earth's climate is cold enough for sheets of ice to cover large areas of the planet.

Catastrophic floods often occur during ice ages. Huge lakes of melted water break through ice dams and water floods over land, carrying boulders and carving out canyons.

There have been times in history when Earth was almost completely covered in ice. Scientists call these periods "SNOWBALL EARTH."

During the last ice age, the area that is NEW YORK CITY today was covered in a glacier that would have easily covered the tallest skyscrapers many times over.

During the last ice age, so much of Earth's water was trapped in glaciers that the sea level was 394 feet (120 m) lower than it is today.

Long Island, Martha's Vineyard, and Cape Cod were all created in the last ice age when glaciers dragged large areas of rock into the ocean.

GIGANTIC JUPITER

Gas giant Jupiter is the **FIFTH FARTHEST PLANET** from the Sun and the largest in our solar system.

Jupiter is more than twice as big as all the other planets in the solar system combined.

The GREAT RED SPOT on Jupiter is a giant swirling storm that is as big as two Earths!

EVEN THOUGH JUPITER IS MORE THAN 365 MILLION MILES (588 MILLION KM) FROM EARTH, YOU CAN EASILY SEE IT IN THE NIGHT SKY.

One of Jupiter's moons, **EUROPA**, may have more water under its icy shell than all the water on Earth.

IO, one of Jupiter's moons, has more volcanic eruptions than any other planet or moon in the solar system.

Because of Jupiter's strong gravity, a kid who weighs 70 pounds (32 kg) on Earth would weigh 168 pounds (76 kg) on Jupiter.

WEB SPINNERS

SPIDERS are eight-legged predatory invertebrates that spin silk, which some spiders use to make webs.

GROUND SPIDERS get food by shooting sticky silk at their targets.

FISHING SPIDERS can walk on water and dive to catch their prey.

HUNTSMAN SPIDERS live in colonies. The older spiders share prey with their little brothers and sisters.

Male **REDBACK WIDOW SPIDERS** want to be eaten after mating and purposely jump into the females' mouths.

Some **TRIANGLE WEAVERS** use their webs like slingshots and fling themselves—and their webs—at nearby bugs they want to eat.

EARTH'S MAGNETIC PERSONALITY

Earth is a gigantic magnet with north and south magnetic poles and a **MAGNETIC FIELD**.

The **MAGNETIC NORTH POLE** keeps moving around. A few decades ago it was in northern Canada, but now it's closer to northern Russia.

Some bacteria produce **MAGNETITE** in their single-celled bodies. The magnetite is attracted to Earth's magnetic field, so the bacteria always point north—like living compasses.

Throughout Earth's history, the magnetic pole has switched back and forth from being near the North Pole to being near the South Pole.

Animals like **SEA TURTLES**, salmon, and many birds use the Earth's magnetic field to find their way during migrations.

THE HUMAN MACHINE

YOUR BODY is like a living machine with organs, blood, and even tiny microbes that all help keep you alive.

Your body's largest organ is your **SKIN**.

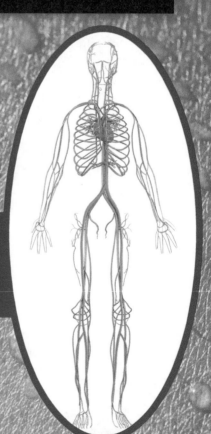

If a kid stretched out all their blood vessels into one long line, they could circle Earth three times. That's more than 60,000 miles (96,560 km)!

Your **BRAIN** is only 2 percent of your body weight, but it uses 20 percent of the energy from the food you eat.

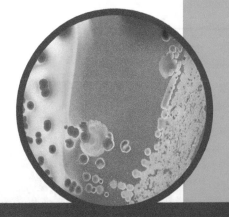

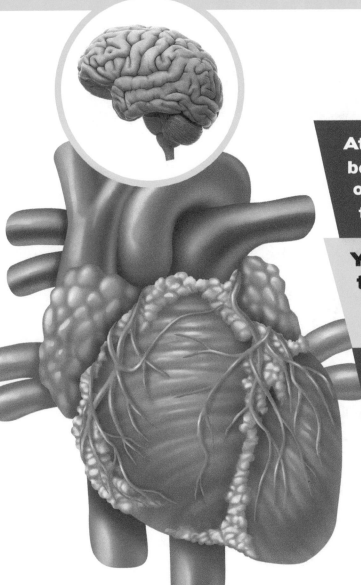

At least half the cells in your body are **BACTERIA** and other microscopic living things called **MICROBES**.

Your **HEART** beats 100,000 times every day and is the only muscle that never rests.

YOUR BODY IS
65 percent oxygen,
18 percent carbon,
10 percent hydrogen,
and 3 percent nitrogen.
The remaining 4 percent
is a mixture of other
elements.

25

MARVELOUS
MOUNTAINS

MOUNTAINS are large, rocky formations that rise steeply from the surrounding area.

The **HIMALAYA MOUNTAINS** grow about 0.4 inch (1 cm) taller every year.

The tallest mountain on Earth is **MAUNA KEA** in Hawaii. From its base on the ocean floor to its peak, it is 33,500 feet (10,210 m) tall.

The **GUADALUPE MOUNTAINS** in Texas are very tall fossilized remains of ancient coral reefs.

The world's longest mountain range is underwater. The mid-ocean ridge stretches 40,389 miles (65,000 km) around the planet.

AMAZING ANIMALS OF THE
CENOZOIC

The **CENOZOIC ERA** stretches from 66 million years ago to today. It started after the mass extinction that wiped out most dinosaurs.

LIVYATAN WHALES lived about 12 million years ago and had 12-inch-long (30 cm) sharp teeth they used to eat other whales and possibly sharks, too.

Huge **TERROR BIRDS** were South America's dominant predator for 60 million years. Some were taller than 9 feet (2.7 m)!

ANCIENT HORSES were the size of dogs.

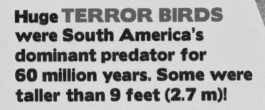

During the last 100,000 years, **GIANT SLOTHS**, giant kangaroos, giant beavers, and giant bears all walked the earth.

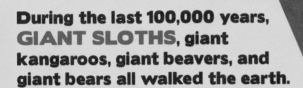

GRASSLAND HABITATS did not appear on Earth until about 20 million years ago. Once they did, herds of grass-eating animals like bison and pronghorns evolved.

SUNSATIONAL!

The Sun is the yellow **DWARF STAR** in the center of our solar system.

The Sun is so big that 1.3 million Earths could fit inside it.

The Sun is a ball of gas made up mostly of two elements. It is 91 percent hydrogen and 8.9 percent helium.

THE SUN'S CORE CAN REACH 27 MILLION DEGREES FAHRENHEIT (15 MILLION DEGREES CELSIUS).

The Sun is 93 million miles (150 km) away from the Earth. It takes the Sun's light 8 minutes and 20 seconds to reach us.

Five billion years from now, the Sun will start running out of fuel and turn into a **RED GIANT** star that may consume the inner solar system.

H₂-OH!

WATER is a colorless liquid made of hydrogen and oxygen.

EARTH'S OCEAN HOLDS 97 PERCENT OF ALL THE WATER ON THE PLANET.

All the water on Earth has been recycling for billions of years. That means water you have drunk may have once been drunk by a *Tyrannosaurus rex* or Marie Curie.

Water is attracted to static electricity. If you hold a staticky balloon near a trickle of water, the water will bend toward the balloon.

Water molecules are attracted to each other and to surfaces. This is what creates water drops and surface tension, or the "skin" on the water's surface.

If the 0.001 percent of Earth's water in the atmosphere all came down as rain at once, it would cover the entire planet in 1 inch (2.5 cm) of water.

IT'S SHOCKING!

LIGHTNING is an intense spark of electricity that moves between clouds or from clouds to the ground.

Around the world, there are 50 to 100 lightning strikes every second.

Lightning can heat the air around it to temperatures five times hotter than the surface of the Sun—about 50,000°F (27,760°C)!

SOME LIGHTNING BOLTS CAN TRAVEL 25 MILES (40 KM) ACROSS THE SKY.

BALL LIGHTNING is a sphere of electricity that seems to float along the ground for a few seconds.

A lightning bolt can contain one billion volts of electricity—about the same number of volts as 667 million AA batteries.

MEET THE
DOLPHINS

DOLPHINS are marine mammals with long snouts, a blowhole, and fins.

ONLY HALF OF A DOLPHIN'S BRAIN SLEEPS AT A TIME. THE OTHER HALF STAYS AWAKE SO IT CAN TELL THE DOLPHIN TO RISE TO THE SURFACE TO TAKE BREATHS.

Some dolphins that live near muddy wetlands chase fish to the shore, then flop onto land to eat their prey.

Male Amazon river dolphins are pink because they fight with other males over females. The pink comes from scar tissue!

One of the dolphin's closest relatives is the **HIPPOPOTAMUS**.

Dolphins shed and replace their skin cells about once every two hours. This keeps them smooth so they can swim faster.

IT'S IN THE BLOOD!

In animals, **BLOOD** carries nutrients, heat, and oxygen to all the body's cells, while removing waste.

The average person's body makes 2 to 3 million blood cells every second.

White blood cells make up a little less than 1 percent of your blood. Their job is to seek and destroy harmful bacteria, viruses, parasites, and other germs.

NINETY-FIVE PERCENT OF BLOOD CELLS ARE MADE BY THE MARROW INSIDE OUR BONES.

VAMPIRE BATS can't survive more than two nights without a blood meal.

SEA STARS and **SEA URCHINS** don't have blood. They use seawater to carry food and oxygen to their cells and remove waste.

The **ANTARCTIC BLACKFIN ICEFISH** has clear blood.

SMALL, BUT MIGHTY!

BACTERIA are microscopic single-cell organisms. They are the simplest living things.

Some bacteria species generate electricity when they breathe and can even power a battery.

Our guts have bacteria that make **VITAMIN K** for our bodies to use. Without this bacteria, we would not survive.

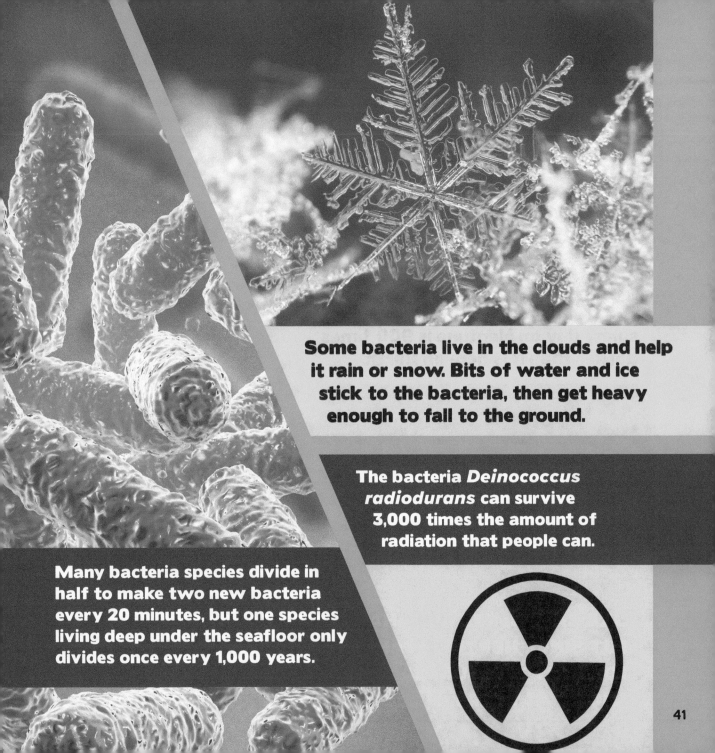

Some bacteria live in the clouds and help it rain or snow. Bits of water and ice stick to the bacteria, then get heavy enough to fall to the ground.

The bacteria *Deinococcus radiodurans* can survive 3,000 times the amount of radiation that people can.

Many bacteria species divide in half to make two new bacteria every 20 minutes, but one species living deep under the seafloor only divides once every 1,000 years.

THE OTHER BLUE PLANET

NEPTUNE is the farthest planet from the Sun in our solar system.

Because Neptune is 2.8 billion miles (4.5 billion km) away from the Sun, a sunny day on Neptune is 900 times darker than it is here on Earth.

Neptune winds can blow at speeds of 1,200 miles (2,000 km) per hour—the fastest in the solar system!

LIKE EARTH, NEPTUNE HAS FOUR SEASONS, BUT SINCE NEPTUNE TAKES 165 EARTH YEARS TO ORBIT THE SUN, EACH SEASON LASTS ABOUT 41 YEARS.

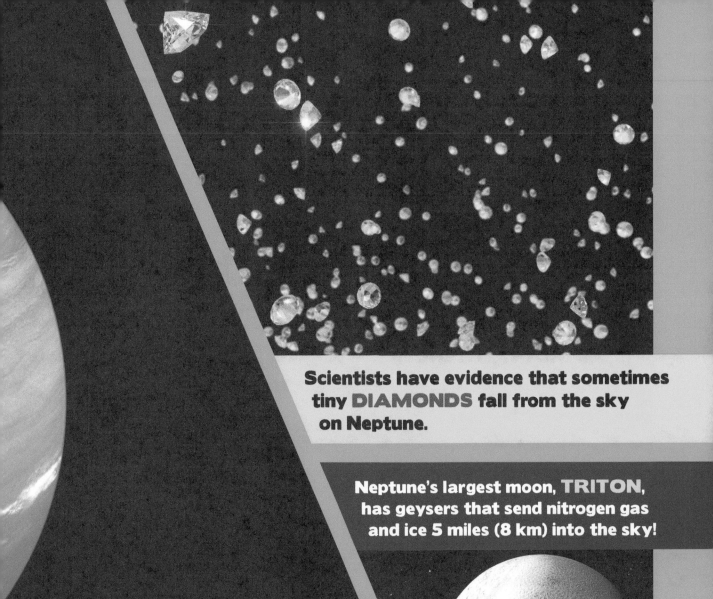

Scientists have evidence that sometimes tiny **DIAMONDS** fall from the sky on Neptune.

Neptune's largest moon, **TRITON**, has geysers that send nitrogen gas and ice 5 miles (8 km) into the sky!

INTO THE DEEP

Found in the ocean, **TRENCHES** are the deepest places on Earth's surface.

The **MARIANA TRENCH** is the deepest trench on Earth. It extends more than 6 miles (9.6 km) below sea level.

The pressure at the bottom of the Mariana Trench is more than 16,000 pounds (7,200 km) per square inch. That's like having a small school bus parked on every square inch of your body.

TRENCHES ARE PLACES WHERE THE ROCKY SEAFLOOR SINKS INTO THE HOT MANTLE. AS THIS HAPPENS, THE ROCKS MELT AND RISE UP TO FORM VOLCANOES.

Even the Mariana Trench has litter in it. Scientists found a SPAM container on the bottom and many small animals that had swallowed tiny plastic garbage.

VOLCANIC ROCKS

IGNEOUS ROCKS are made when magma, or lava, turns solid.

PUMICE is a type of igneous rock that floats. In 2019, a volcano in the ocean erupted so much pumice that it covered 200 square miles (322 square km) of ocean.

The oldest known rocks on Earth are 4.4-billion-year-old igneous rocks in the **JACK HILLS OF AUSTRALIA.**

The most common rock in Earth's crust is an igneous rock called **BASALT** that is created by volcanic eruptions.

When lava erupts underwater, it immediately cools into large beanbag-shaped rocks called **PILLOW LAVA.**

OBSIDIAN is a natural glass that forms when lava cools really quickly. Obsidian edges are so sharp that surgeons use scalpel blades made from it.

FLOWER FRIENDS

Plants use flower pollen to make seeds. **POLLINATORS** feed from the flowers and deliver pollen from one plant to another.

BEES AND OTHER BUGS ARE ATTRACTED TO ULTRAVIOLET LIGHT PATTERNS AND SHADES OF BLUE ON FLOWERS THAT HUMANS CAN'T SEE.

Some flowers can "**HEAR**" bees buzzing nearby. When they hear a pollinator, the plants make their nectar taste sweeter to attract the bee.

CORPSE FLOWERS smell like rotting meat to attract carrion-eating flies and beetles that help spread their pollen.

Plants like **AGAVE** and **WILD BANANAS** have specially shaped flowers that make bats' echolocation noises louder so the bats don't miss the opportunity to pollinate the flowers.

VENUS FLY TRAPS eat many types of insects, but not the sweat bees, checkered beetles, and other pollinators that visit their flowers.

A **HUMMINGBIRD**'s tongue is so long that it stays coiled inside the hummingbird's head when it's not being used to eat nectar out of flowers.

49

IT'S INVISIBLE!

ULTRAVIOLET (UV) LIGHT is a form of radiation. Humans cannot see it, but some animals can.

Some animals, like frogs, **SQUID**, and flying squirrels, reflect ultraviolet light through a process called fluorescence and glow under UV light.

The ultraviolet light from the Sun is dangerous, but a gas called **OZONE** in the upper atmosphere blocks 95 percent of dangerous UV radiation from reaching us.

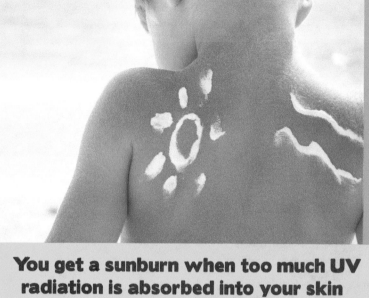

You get a sunburn when too much UV radiation is absorbed into your skin and damages its inner layer.

Our skin produces a pigment called **MELANIN**. Melanin absorbs UV light and prevents it from damaging skin cells.

UV light helps our skin make the vitamin D we need to stay healthy. It takes 10 to 15 minutes in the Sun for your body to make all the vitamin D you need for the day.

COLORFUL SPACE CLOUDS

A **NEBULA** is a huge cloud of gas and dust in outer space where some stars are born.

In 1054, Chinese astronomers saw the supernova explosion that created the **CRAB NEBULA**.

Our own solar system formed 4.5 billion years ago from a solar nebula.

Scientists have found about 1,100 points of light in the "**PILLARS OF CREATION**" formation in the Eagle Nebula that are likely newborn stars.

The **BUTTERFLY NEBULA** is being created by a dying star that is spewing gas and dust into space.

The **GHOST NEBULA** has an eerie glow because it is being blasted with radiation from a blue giant star with the energy of 34,000 suns.

AMAZING ANIMALS OF THE
CRETACEOUS

The **CRETACEOUS PERIOD** took place from 145 to 66 million years ago. It was part of the age of the dinosaurs.

The age of dinosaurs lasted from 230 million to 66 million years ago. *TYRANNOSAURUS REX* lived only during the last couple million years of that time (68 to 66 million years ago).

Therizinosaurus was a dinosaur whose long, sharp claws were like 3-foot (1 m) swords.

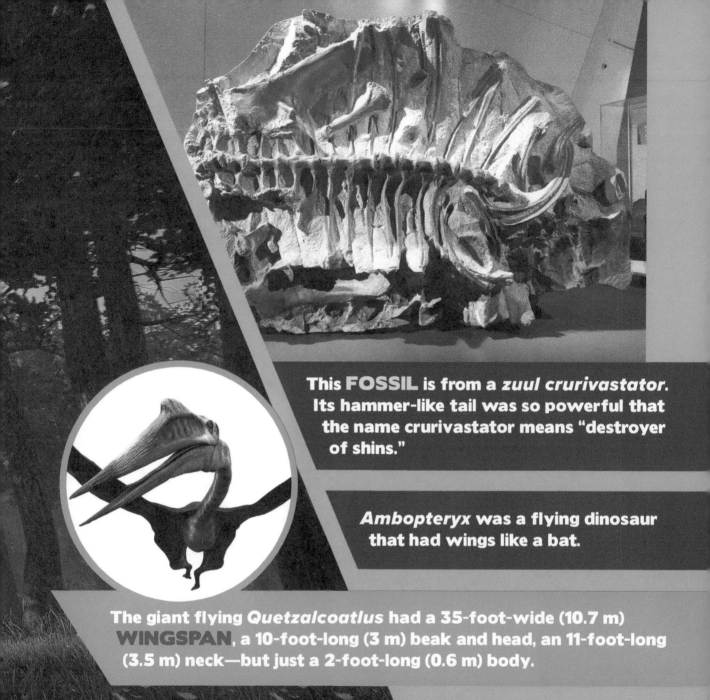

This **FOSSIL** is from a *zuul crurivastator*. Its hammer-like tail was so powerful that the name crurivastator means "destroyer of shins."

Ambopteryx was a flying dinosaur that had wings like a bat.

The giant flying *Quetzalcoatlus* had a 35-foot-wide (10.7 m) **WINGSPAN**, a 10-foot-long (3 m) beak and head, an 11-foot-long (3.5 m) neck—but just a 2-foot-long (0.6 m) body.

GLITTERING GOLD

Gold is a **YELLOW METAL** that is one of the heavier elements.

Just one ounce of gold can be beaten into a 300-square-foot (91 square m) sheet—enough to cover the floor of a one-car garage.

Gold is made when neutron stars collide. The tremendous energy of a collision can produce enough gold to fill 200 Earths.

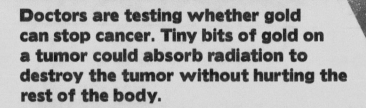
Doctors are testing whether gold can stop cancer. Tiny bits of gold on a tumor could absorb radiation to destroy the tumor without hurting the rest of the body.

ALL THE GOLD ON EARTH MAY HAVE BEEN BROUGHT HERE BY ANCIENT METEORITES.

Gold is a metal that doesn't rust, corrode, or tarnish. A tiny amount of gold is used in each smartphone to make long-lasting electrical components.

WHEN EARTH SHAKES

An **EARTHQUAKE** happens when pieces of Earth's crust grind past each other.

Earthquakes can cause soil to act like water and make cars sink into the ground.

Scientists found NEMATODE WORMS living in rocks 0.9 miles (1.4 km) below the ground in South Africa. They were brought there by an earthquake that created deep fractures in the rock.

The asteroid impact that led to the extinction of most dinosaurs caused tremendous earthquakes around the world that were more intense than any earthquake experienced by humans.

Not all earthquakes are quick and violent. During slow earthquakes, the land shifts gently over a period of weeks.

Landslides from earthquakes in the Pacific Northwest of North America dammed up rivers. The dams created lakes that have underwater "ghost forests" filled with drowned trees.

59

FREAKY FROGS

Frogs are **TAILLESS AMPHIBIANS** with large hind legs and live their lives part in water and part on land.

Some frogs, like **SPRING PEEPERS**, freeze almost solid in the winter and then thaw out and return to normal life in the spring.

The **DEVIL FROG** lived 70 to 66 million years ago and grew to be the size of a watermelon.

GLIDING LEAF FROGS CAN SPREAD OUT THE SKIN BETWEEN THEIR TOES TO ALLOW THEM TO GLIDE THROUGH THE AIR FROM TREE TO TREE.

A STRAWBERRY POISON DART FROG dad carries his tadpole baby up a tree on his back. He puts the tadpole in a flower full of rainwater where it can safely grow up.

When a frog flicks its tongue, its special saliva acts like a liquid to keep the tongue flexible. When it smacks a bug, the saliva becomes a sticky solid to grasp the prey.

61

THE ATMOSPHERE AROUND US

The **ATMOSPHERE** is the layer of gases—including the air around us—that covers the surface of the Earth.

DUST in the atmosphere provides iron and other necessary nutrients to tiny plant plankton. The plankton feed everything else in the ocean.

The atmosphere may not look like a habitat, but it is filled with bacteria, fungi, and microbes.

Before photosynthesis started 2.5 billion years ago, there was barely any oxygen in the atmosphere.

The atmosphere is heavy! If you weighed just the air inside the EMPIRE STATE BUILDING, it would weigh 2,985,900 pounds (1,355,000 kg).

Ninety-nine percent of our atmosphere is made up of just two gases: nitrogen (78 percent) and oxygen (21 percent).

Without tiny amounts of greenhouse gases like carbon dioxide and methane, the average temperature on Earth would be a chilly 0°F (-18°C).

METEOROIDS, METEORS, AND METEORITES

A **METEOR** is a **METEOROID**, or space rock, that burns up in Earth's atmosphere. Meteoroids that land on Earth are called **METEORITES**.

In 1954, a woman in Alabama was hit in the hip by a meteorite that crashed through her roof.

Some meteorites found on Earth are actually chunks of the planet Mars.

About 97,000 pounds (44,000 kg) of meteoroids enter Earth's atmosphere every day.

In 1908, a 120-foot (37 m) meteor hurtled over Tunguska, Siberia, and released so much energy that it knocked over 80 million trees.

There is a 53-mile-wide (85 km) crater in the Chesapeake Bay, left behind by a meteorite that struck the area about 35 million years ago.

JUST JELLYFISH

JELLYFISH are aquatic animals with stinging tentacles and bodies that are about 95 percent water.

Jellyfish are animals without hearts, brains, blood, or skeletons. They are basically just floating stomachs that can reproduce themselves.

UPSIDE-DOWN JELLYFISH catch their tiny prey by hitting them with balls of stinging mucus.

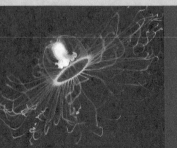

An adult *Turritopsis dohrnii* jellyfish can turn back into a baby, grow to adulthood, then start the process again, possibly forever.

A LION'S MANE JELLYFISH can grow to 120 feet (54 m)—about as long as 2.5 school buses.

A CUP OF JELLYFISH CONTAINS ONLY FIVE CALORIES.

Scientists have found jellyfish fossils in China that are 518 million years old.

PHENOMENAL FIRE

FIRE is a chemical reaction between oxygen and a fuel—it produces heat, light, and smoke.

EARTH IS THE ONLY PLANET IN THE SOLAR SYSTEM THAT HAS ENOUGH OXYGEN IN ITS ATMOSPHERE TO ALLOW FIRE TO BURN.

Lightning bolts cause as many as 20,000 fires every day.

LODGEPOLE PINE TREE
PINECONES WON'T OPEN TO RELEASE THEIR SEEDS UNLESS THEY ARE HEATED BY FIRE.

HYDROGEN is a gas that can catch on fire. The Hindenburg airship tragically exploded because it was filled with hydrogen.

ZAP!

STATIC ELECTRICITY happens when something has extra electrons that jump to a positively charged object.

When you rub your hair with a balloon, the hairs stand up because they all have a **POSITIVE CHARGE** and push each other away.

If you rub electrons from your hair onto a balloon, you can use the balloon to roll an empty soda can across a floor.

Being zapped by static electricity can be painful. The sparks have enough energy to **IGNITE FIREWORKS**.

LASER PRINTERS put extra electrons on paper in the shape of letters. The positively charged toner then clings to the shapes.

Static electricity is more shocking in winter because **HUMIDITY ATTRACTS ELECTRONS**. Summer's moist air pulls extra electrons off you before you can get shocked.

WALLS OF WATER

A **TSUNAMI** is a huge wave created in the open ocean by an underwater earthquake, landslide, or volcanic eruption.

Tsunamis can travel more than 500 miles (800 km) per hour across the open ocean—as fast as a jet plane flies.

In 1700, a tsunami that formed near the Pacific Northwest coast traveled 5,000 miles (8,047 km) across the ocean and flooded Japanese coastal towns.

Akita
Sado
Niigata
Sendai
JAPAN
Nagano
Honshu
TOKYO
Tottori
Kyoto   Lake Biwa
Kobe   Nagoya   Yokohama
Hiroshima   Osaka   Hamamatsu
Matsuyama
Shikoku
Nanpo Islands
Islands
Mount Rocks

The 2011 tsunami in Japan swept 5 million tons of debris into the ocean. Some made it all the way to the United States.

The huge asteroid that crashed into the Gulf of Mexico 66 million years ago created tsunamis that may have been 5,000 feet (1,524 m) high!

Tsunamis are often caused by earthquakes in marine trenches. The Pacific Ocean has so many trenches that 80 percent of tsunamis happen there.

THE RED PLANET

MARS is a rocky red planet that is smaller than Earth. It is the fourth planet from the Sun.

Mars has ice covering its poles. Scientists have also discovered an underground lake of liquid water beneath the Martian ice cap.

Mars has canyons, gorges, and even the remains of beaches. This proves there were once rivers on Mars that flowed to **MARTIAN OCEANS.**

DEIMOS

PHOBOS

Mars has two moons, **DEIMOS** and **PHOBOS**, that are less than 17 miles (27 km) across.

Mars once had a thick atmosphere, but as the planet's magnetic field weakened over time, the Sun's solar wind blew almost all the atmosphere away.

PHOBOS keeps getting closer to Mars and may crash into the red planet in 50 million years.

OLYMPUS MONS, one of Mars's volcanoes, is the biggest volcano in the solar system. It is 100 times larger than Mauna Loa, Earth's largest volcano.

TREE-MENDOUS TREES

TREES are tall woody plants, covered in bark, with leaves that grow on the top.

A **BAOBAB TREE** can store 31,000 gallons (117,347 l) of water in its trunk.

Golf-ball-sized avocado seeds evolved to be pooped out by extinct giant ground sloths to spread new trees to other places.

TREES USE A NETWORK OF ROOTS AND FUNGI IN THE SOIL TO SHARE NUTRIENTS WITH OTHER TREES.

REDWOODS, the tallest trees in the world, need to live by the coast because they get as much as **40** percent of the water they need from ocean fog.

GOODBYE, DINOSAURS

Scientists have evidence that an asteroid crashed into the Gulf of Mexico 66 million years ago and caused a mass extinction. Mass extinctions are when most of the species on Earth go extinct in a short period of time.

About 75 percent of all species went extinct because of the asteroid's impact, including dinosaurs, many plants, and most ocean species.

The asteroid was so hot that its heat would have killed dinosaurs hundreds of miles away in what's now Texas.

Birds are dinosaurs that survived the mass extinction. Today, there are 10,000 of these dinosaur species alive on Earth.

SULFUR PARTICLES were blown into the atmosphere at impact and blocked the sunlight for years. This was the main cause of extinction.

When the asteroid hit Earth, it blasted chunks of rock skyward with so much energy that some may have landed on the Moon.

79

TAKE YOUR VITAMINS!

VITAMINS are nutrients that living things need to grow and survive.

POLAR BEAR LIVERS HAVE ENOUGH VITAMIN A IN THEM TO BE POISONOUS FOR HUMANS TO EAT.

VITAMINS A, D, E, and K can be stored in your fat for later use. The rest of the vitamins leave your body when you pee, so you need to eat them regularly.

People who go too long without getting enough **VITAMIN A** can go blind.

VITAMIN K helps your blood clot when you have a cut.

VITAMIN B₁₂ may make us happy. Studies show that some people with depression do not have enough B₁₂ in their diets. You can get vitamin B₁₂ from foods like eggs, fish, and cheese.

SEDIMENTARY ROCKS

SEDIMENTARY ROCKS are usually formed in the ocean or in lakes and rivers when grains of sand, mud, pebbles, and shells are pressed together over time.

LIMESTONE is made of seashells. Anywhere it is found—like Kansas or the tops of the Himalaya Mountains—used to be under the ocean.

Most **FOSSILS** are found in sedimentary rocks.

SHALE can be used as a fossil fuel because it is made of tiny grains of rock and the remains of ancient living things.

The asteroid impact 66 million years ago blasted trillions of tons of rock into the air. The rocks mixed together to form a sedimentary rock called **BRECCIA**.

When **MAGMA** rises through limestone, the limestone dissolves into carbon dioxide and creates a volcano with a lot of gas.

THE MAGNIFICENT MILKY WAY

OUR SOLAR SYSTEM is located in the Milky Way galaxy.

The Milky Way consumes smaller galaxies that get too close. Astronomers found 11 star streams in the Milky Way that are remnants of galaxies it ate.

We don't know for sure how many stars are in the Milky Way, but scientists predict there are hundreds of billions.

In about 4 billion years, the Milky Way is going to collide with the ANDROMEDA GALAXY, our closest spiral galaxy neighbor.

Every star we see in the night sky is in the MILKY WAY GALAXY.

Everything in the Milky Way revolves around a supermassive black hole named SAGITTARIUS A*. It takes our Solar System 250 million years to complete one orbit.

ON THE HUNT

PREDATORS are animals that hunt other live animals to eat.

SPERM WHALES dive down more than 1.5 miles (2.4 km) to hunt for the 40-foot-long (12 m) giant squid that live there.

Today, **ANCHOVIES** are tiny fish we put on pizza, but 40 to 50 million years ago, there were saber-toothed predatory anchovies that were 3 feet (0.9 m) long.

MANTIS SHRIMP are just a few inches long, but their "arms" pack a punch strong enough to break a crab's shell, or even glass!

SPINOSAURUS was a 50-foot-long (15.2 m) land predator that used its paddle-like tail and crocodile mouth to capture prey underwater.

The **ALLIGATOR SNAPPING TURTLE** lures prey by wiggling a piece of skin on its tongue that looks just like a tasty worm.

LISTEN UP!

SOUND is caused by vibrations that move through air or other substances.

IF A JET IS FLYING FASTER THAN THE SPEED OF SOUND, YOU WON'T HEAR ITS ENGINES UNTIL IT PASSES YOU.

Sound waves travel 1,125 feet (343 m) per second through air, but they speed up to 16,400 feet (5,000 m) per second through iron.

OUTER SPACE is completely silent. It has no air for sound to move through, so vibrations can't make sound waves.

Sound waves can bounce off solid things and create an **ECHO**. Bats and dolphins use the echoes from sounds they make to find prey.

When you talk, your lungs move air over your throat's vocal folds, making them vibrate. The vibrations send sound waves—your voice—out of your mouth.

JOURNEY TO THE CENTER OF THE EARTH

The **CORE** of a planet is its innermost layer—its dense center.

INNER CORE

OUTER CORE

Earth's outer core is liquid, but its hotter inner core is solid because it is under so much pressure.

Scientists think Earth's magnetic field is created by the liquid outer core spinning around the solid inner core.

Earth's core formed when the planet's temperature reached 2,800°F (1,538°C). That's when Earth's iron turned liquid and sank to its center.

Earth's core is a nuclear furnace that can reach 10,800°F (5,982°C).

If Earth's core cooled, the planet would lose its magnetic field and living things would no longer be protected from dangerous solar wind and flares.

IRON, MAN!

Iron is a gray **METAL** that is attracted to magnets.

When iron reacts with oxygen, it turns red. Rusty nails, the planet Mars, and your blood are all red because they have iron in them.

Your body needs iron to make proteins such as hemoglobin, which carries oxygen to our cells.

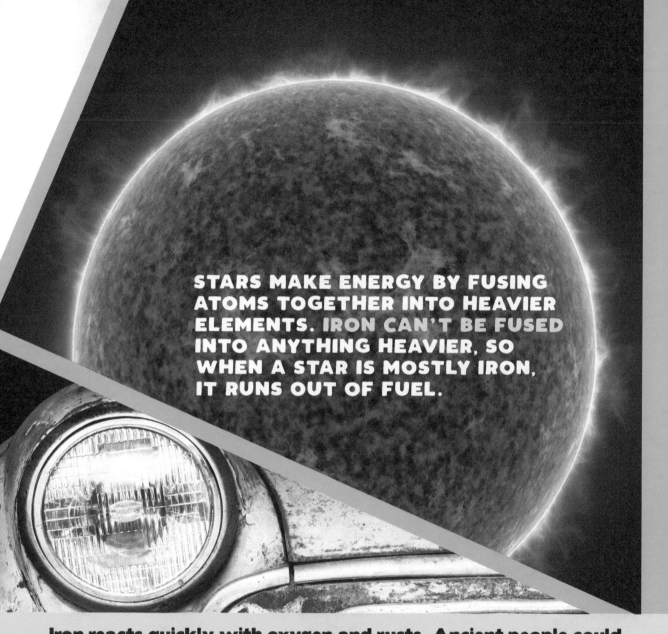

STARS MAKE ENERGY BY FUSING
ATOMS TOGETHER INTO HEAVIER
ELEMENTS. IRON CAN'T BE FUSED
INTO ANYTHING HEAVIER, SO
WHEN A STAR IS MOSTLY IRON,
IT RUNS OUT OF FUEL.

Iron reacts quickly with oxygen and rusts. Ancient people could
only get unrusty iron for their tools from inside meteorites.

CRAFTY CAMOUFLAGE AND MIMICRY

An animal with **CAMOUFLAGE** blends into its environment to hide from predators or prey. **MIMICRY** is when an animal looks like something its predators want to avoid, or like something that attracts prey.

GIANT MALAYSIAN LEAF INSECTS LOOK AND MOVE EXACTLY LIKE THE LEAVES THEY EAT.

CUTTLEFISH can change the color, texture, and shape of their skin to match their surroundings.

DECORATOR CRABS

ATTACH BITS OF SHELL, SEAWEED, AND EVEN OTHER ANIMALS, SUCH AS SEA ANEMONES, TO THEIR SHELLS TO MAKE THEM LOOK LIKE THE SEAFLOOR.

Some **CATERPILLARS** avoid becoming a bird's lunch by looking exactly like the last thing a bird wants to eat: bird poop.

GOLDENROD CRAB SPIDERS can change their colors to look like yellow or white flowers to hide from the pollinating insects they want to eat.

COOL COMETS

A **COMET** is a ball of ice and dust in space that has a long, glowing tail.

THERE IS EVIDENCE THAT THE WATER ON EARTH CAME FROM COMETS THAT BOMBARDED THE PLANET AND MELTED TO FILL UP THE OCEANS.

In 1770, **LEXELL'S COMET** came within 1.4 million miles (2.2 million km) of Earth—the closest comet flyby in human history.

METEOR SHOWERS happen when Earth orbits through dust left behind by a comet. The dust ignites in the atmosphere to create shooting stars.

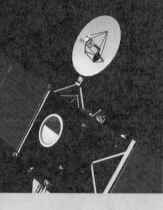

In 2014, the European Space Agency's Rosetta probe was the first spacecraft to ever visit a comet.

Some of the ingredients for life on Earth may have come from comets. The space probe **ROSETTA** found chemical compounds on the comet that living things need.

97

HOT, HOT, HOT!

HOT PEPPERS, also known as chile peppers, are actually berries that produce a burning sensation when eaten.

The "hotness" of hot peppers is actually pain. Chemicals in hot peppers called *capsaicinoids* trigger pain sensors in our mouths.

People like hot peppers because our bodies fight the pain by releasing feel-good hormones called ENDORPHINS.

Birds don't feel the pain of hot peppers. They happily eat them and spread the pepper seeds when they poop.

DRAGON'S BREATH chile peppers are hot enough to make a person stop breathing!

TREE SHREWS love eating chile peppers. Peppers don't hurt their mouths like they do with other mammals.

RIVERS OF ICE

A **GLACIER** is a huge mass of ice and snow that moves very slowly over land.

Some of the oldest GLACIER ICE on Earth is 2.7 million years old.

Glacier ice is a type of **METAMORPHIC ROCK.**

Some glaciers look pink in the summer because PINK ALGAE grows on their surfaces.

If all the ice on land melted, the sea level around the world would rise 230 feet (70 m). Florida, the Netherlands, and many other places would be underwater.

PLENTY OF PLANKTON

PLANKTON are mostly microscopic animals or plants that live in water and are not strong enough to swim against the current.

Plant plankton produce **50 percent of** the world's food every day through photosynthesis.

Trillions of animal plankton hide in the deep ocean during the day and rise to feed on plant plankton at night. This is the biggest animal migration in the world.

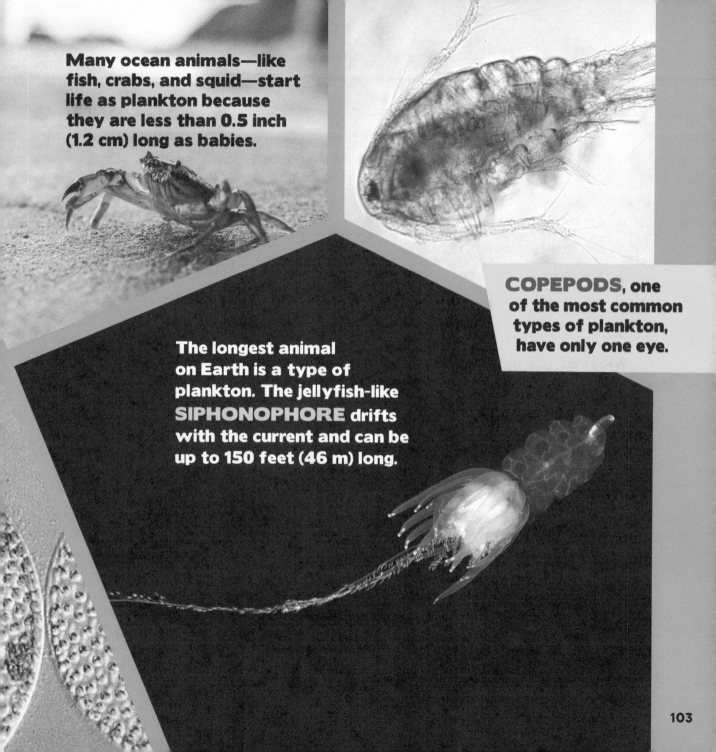

Many ocean animals—like fish, crabs, and squid—start life as plankton because they are less than 0.5 inch (1.2 cm) long as babies.

COPEPODS, one of the most common types of plankton, have only one eye.

The longest animal on Earth is a type of plankton. The jellyfish-like SIPHONOPHORE drifts with the current and can be up to 150 feet (46 m) long.

NIFTY NITROGEN

NITROGEN is a colorless, odorless gas that makes up 78 percent of Earth's atmosphere.

Most of the air around us is nitrogen gas, so when we inhale and exhale, we are breathing mostly nitrogen.

Nitrogen is found in all proteins, which living things need to build tissues and to keep their cells running.

BACTERIA IN THE SOIL TURN NITROGEN GAS INTO AMMONIA THAT PLANTS NEED TO GROW.

If scuba divers come to the surface too fast, they can get "**THE BENDS**." This happens when water-pressure changes create nitrogen gas bubbles in the body.

Nitrogen is a component of **NITRO-GLYCERIN**. As a liquid, nitroglycerin is a dangerous explosive, but as a solid, it is a medicine used to treat heart disease symptoms.

BLAZING-HOT VENUS

VENUS is a rocky planet about the same size as Earth. It is the second planet from the Sun.

Eighty percent of Venus's surface is covered by **VOLCANIC ROCK**. It's possible Venus may still have active volcanoes.

Venus has clouds of sulfuric acid that sometimes fall as rain, but the drops evaporate before they reach the ground.

Venus's atmosphere is 96 percent carbon dioxide and traps so much heat that the planet's surface can be hotter than 880°F (471°C).

Venus rotates in the opposite direction of all the other planets in the solar system, so on Venus the Sun rises in the west and sets in the east.

OCEAN CHIMNEYS

HYDROTHERMAL VENTS are places where magma-heated boiling water rises up out of the seafloor.

The water spewing out of hydrothermal vents can reach temperatures of 700°F (371°C), but the extreme pressure of the deep sea keeps the water from boiling.

MICROBES living in hydrothermal vents turn chemicals in the hot water into food through a process called *chemosynthesis*.

Hot water deposits minerals around the vents to form tall rock chimneys. The biggest chimneys are 180 feet (55 m) tall.

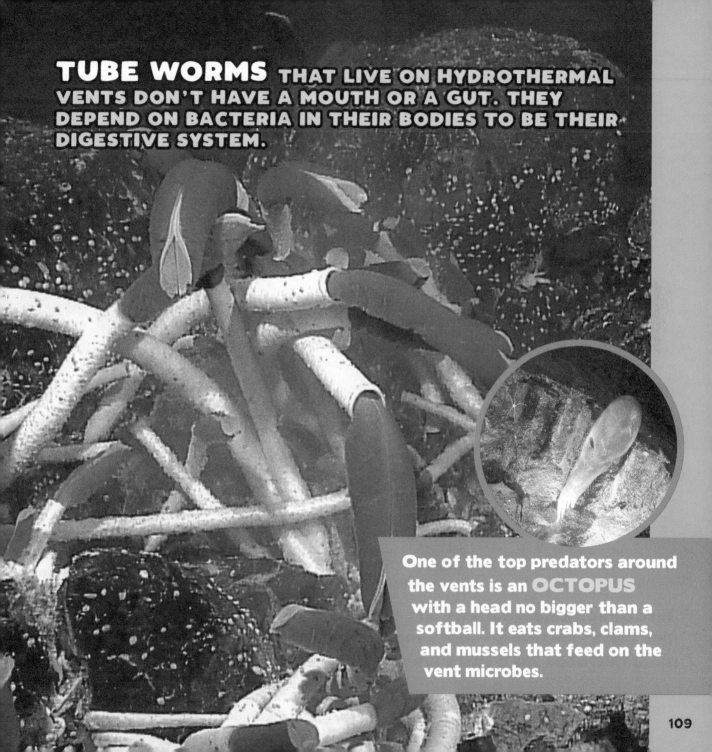

TUBE WORMS THAT LIVE ON HYDROTHERMAL VENTS DON'T HAVE A MOUTH OR A GUT. THEY DEPEND ON BACTERIA IN THEIR BODIES TO BE THEIR DIGESTIVE SYSTEM.

One of the top predators around the vents is an **OCTOPUS** with a head no bigger than a softball. It eats crabs, clams, and mussels that feed on the vent microbes.

BACKYARD SCIENCE

SCIENCE doesn't just happen in space or in the ocean. There are amazing things to discover right near your home.

The *chick-a-dee-dee-dee* call of a **CHICKADEE** is a warning that danger is near. The more "dees" in the song, the more dangerous the bird thinks the threat is.

Just three tablespoons of dirt can contain about nine billion microbes—that's more than 1 billion more microbes than there are people on Earth.

A bee that has found a good new food source will perform a "waggle dance" to tell other bees in the hive exactly where the food is.

Microscopic eight-legged animals called **TARDIGRADES** live in moss or lichens. These tough little creatures can live 30 years without eating or drinking!

SQUIRRELS sometimes pretend to bury nuts in case other animals are watching and are hoping to steal their hidden food.

HOT SPOTS

HOT SPOTS are places on Earth where magma rises up from the mantle for long periods of time. Hot spots can create chains of volcanoes on the surface.

Hot spot volcano eruptions aren't usually explosive. The lava oozes out slowly like a thick stream.

PŪHĀHONU is a new island being formed at the Hawaiian Islands hot spot. It is already the world's biggest volcano.

The **YELLOWSTONE SUPERVOLCANO** is the result of a hot spot.

When a hot spot creates a new island, the weight of the lava rock slowly causes the crust beneath it to sink into the mantle. Eventually, the island will be underwater.

The ocean is filled with underwater mountains—called **SEAMOUNTS**—that were once volcanic islands created by hot spots.

GRAVITY IS GROOVY

GRAVITY is a force that pulls things toward each other. The more massive an object is, the stronger its force of gravity.

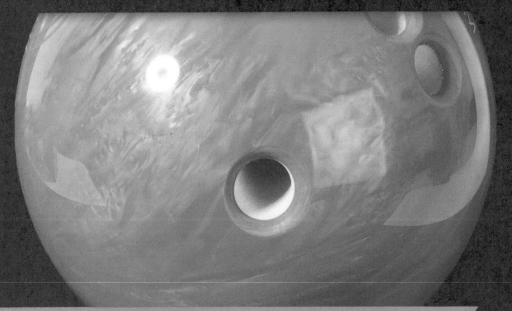

If you dropped a **FEATHER** and a **BOWLING BALL** at the same time on a planet with no atmosphere, they would hit the ground at the same time.

BLACK HOLES have so much gravity that light cannot escape them. The first image of a black hole was a silhouette because we can't see the black hole itself.

Everything with mass has gravity, including you. If you were floating in space, small objects could orbit your body.

If you jumped into a black hole, the gravity at your feet would be so much stronger than the gravity at your head that you would be stretched out like a spaghetti noodle.

115

STRANGE SENSES

An animal's **SENSE ORGANS** collect information from the environment. Some animals have other senses besides sight, sound, touch, smell, and taste.

SATYRINE BUTTERFLIES HAVE VEINS IN THEIR WINGS THAT CARRY SOUNDS TO THEIR EARS.

SHARKS use organs called *ampullae of Lorenzini* to sense electrical fields given off by other animals, including electricity from a nearby fish's heartbeat.

AN **OCTOPUS** CAN SMELL AND TASTE WITH EACH SUCKER ON ITS TENTACLES.

BUMBLEBEES have hairs on their legs that sense a flower's static electricity.

FISH have an organ called a lateral line that senses movement in the water. It alerts them to predators, prey, and fish swimming around them in a school.

SEEING STARS

A **STAR** is large ball of gas that produces light and heat through nuclear fusion.

More than half the stars in the sky may be **BINARY STARS**—two stars that are orbiting each other.

The Milky Way's supermassive black hole blasted a star named **S5-HVS1** out of the galaxy at a speed of 4 million miles (6.4 million km) per hour.

The largest stars, supergiants, can be thousands of times bigger than the Sun. The smallest, neutron stars, are only about 12 miles (19 km) wide.

BETELGEUSE, a red supergiant star, could supernova, or explode, within the next 100,000 years. It is only 700 light years away, so when it does, it will be as bright as the Moon.

There are around 100,000,000,000,000,000,000,000 (100 sextillion) stars in the universe.

HELLO, HELIUM!

HELIUM is a gas that makes up 25 percent of the universe's mass.

If you wanted to lift an 80-pound (36 kg) kid in the air, you would need 2,105 helium balloons.

HELIUM is the second most common element in the universe, but it is hard to collect on Earth. Party balloon shops often have to deal with shortages.

Helium makes up only **0.0005** percent of Earth's atmosphere.

Helium makes your voice sound higher because sound waves travel faster through lighter air.

HYDROGEN and **HELIUM** are both less dense than regular air, which is why balloons filled with them float.

NATURAL PARTNERS

MUTUAL SYMBIOSIS is a partnership where two different species help each other survive.

Some **ACACIA TREES** make food for ants and grow hollow thorns for them to live in. In return, the ants attack the bugs that eat the trees' leaves.

A species of tarantula protects the **DOTTED HUMMING FROG** from predators and the frog eats ants before they eat the tarantula's eggs.

HONEYGUIDE BIRDS IN AFRICA
LEAD A PERSON TO A BEEHIVE, WAIT FOR THE
PERSON TO CRACK THE HIVE OPEN TO COLLECT
HONEY, AND THEN EAT THE BEESWAX LEFT BEHIND.

A species of **AMOEBA** transports bacteria to places where they can thrive. After helping the bacteria spread, the amoeba eats some of them.

Long ago, bacteria moved inside cells to get free food and shelter. They became **MITOCHONDRIA** that provide cells with the energy they need.

SEASONS CHANGE

Earth and other planets have **SEASONS** because each has a tilted axis. As Earth revolves around the Sun, different areas get more daylight than others. This makes the seasons.

The **EQUATOR** is the only place that gets 12 hours of sunlight every day, all year.

VENUS'S AXIS is not tilted that much, so it has one incredibly hot season all the time.

124

EQUATOR

EARTH'S AXIS

When kids in South America are having summer vacation, kids in North America are wearing winter coats.

The North and South Poles have only two seasons: summer and winter. In winter, the Sun never rises, but in the summer the Sun is in the sky 24 hours a day.

SATURN changes color with the seasons. In the winter it looks blue and in summer it looks yellow.

THE RINGED PLANET

SATURN is a gas giant and the sixth planet from the Sun. It has more than 80 moons and the solar system's most impressive rings.

SATURN'S RINGS are made of pieces of ice, dust, and rocks. The pieces range in size from grains of sand to large houses.

The gaps in Saturn's rings are caused by its moons passing through. The moons push particles out of the way as they orbit.

BITS OF SATURN'S RINGS CONSTANTLY RAIN DOWN ON SATURN. IN 100 MILLION YEARS, THE RINGS MAY BE GONE.

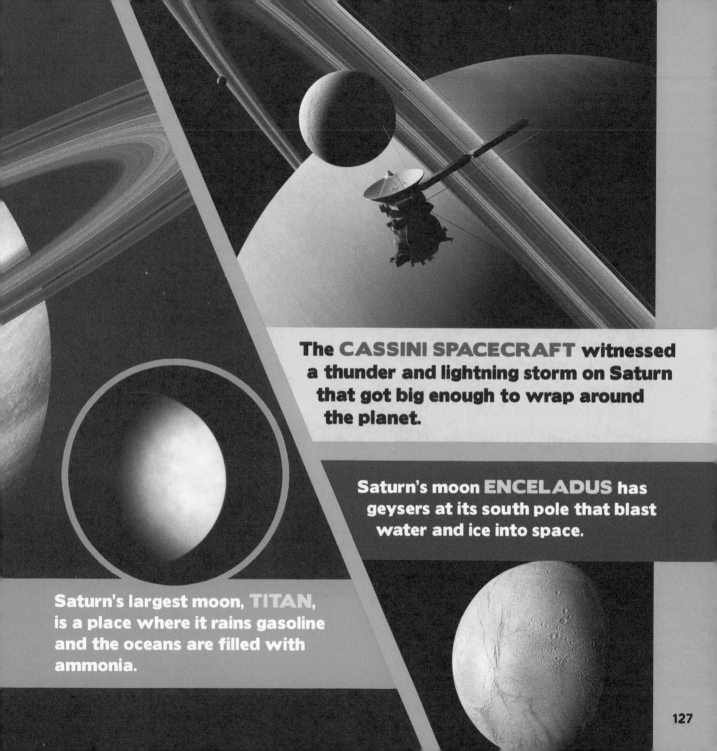

The **CASSINI SPACECRAFT** witnessed a thunder and lightning storm on Saturn that got big enough to wrap around the planet.

Saturn's moon **ENCELADUS** has geysers at its south pole that blast water and ice into space.

Saturn's largest moon, **TITAN**, is a place where it rains gasoline and the oceans are filled with ammonia.

BUILDING BLOCKS

Everything is made of **ATOMS**, the incredibly tiny building blocks of the universe. Atoms combine to form molecules.

Atoms are drawn to look like tiny solar systems, but they do not contain empty space. They are filled with particles and energy.

Scientists have discovered 98 DIFFERENT KINDS OF ATOMS on Earth.

A human who weighs 154 pounds (70 kg) has about 7,000,000,000,000,000,000,000,000,000 (7 octillion) atoms in their body.

Some types of atoms, like oxygen, are so reactive they are almost always joined with other atoms to form molecules. The oxygen we breathe is two oxygen atoms combined (O_2).

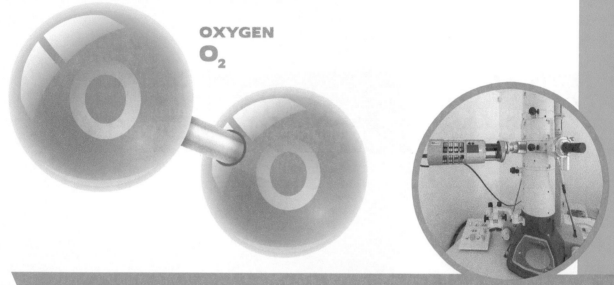

OXYGEN
O_2

Atoms are extremely small, but scientists have seen them using a **TRANSMISSION ELECTRON MICROSCOPE** and magnetic resonance imaging (MRI).

HELIUM and **NEON** are the only types of atoms on Earth that never join other atoms to form molecules.

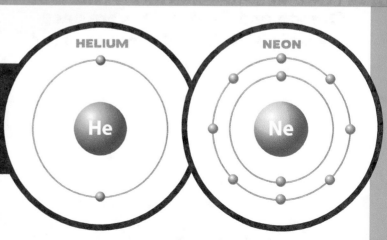

HELIUM

NEON

He

Ne

SHIFTING PLATES

Earth's crust is broken into pieces like a cracked eggshell. These continent-sized pieces of rock are called **PLATES** and they slowly move over time. This movement is called **PLATE TECTONICS**.

The **KLAMATH MOUNTAINS** in Oregon and California were once volcanic islands that were dragged onto land by plate tectonics.

Asteroid impact craters in the ocean don't last long. Plate tectonics move the craters down ocean trenches and into the mantle where they are destroyed.

North american plate

Eurasian plate

North american plate

Caribbean plate

Cocos plate

Arabian plate

Indian plate

Philippine plate

African plate

South american plate

Nazca plate

Australian plate

Scotia plate

Antarctic plate

EASTERN AFRICA has an area where plates are splitting the continent apart. In a few million years, the crack may spread wide enough to create a new ocean.

The **APPALACHIAN MOUNTAINS** were created when the North American and African plates collided 270 million years ago and pushed up rocks.

VERY STRANGE VIRUSES

VIRUSES are germs that are not actually alive. They are basically just DNA (a protein that is like a computer code that tells cells what to do) inside a case. They need to use other cells to reproduce.

Bacteria can get viruses, called *bacteriophages*, that make them sick.

Though some viruses look like ROBOTIC SPIDERS, they do not have legs or any way to move on their own.

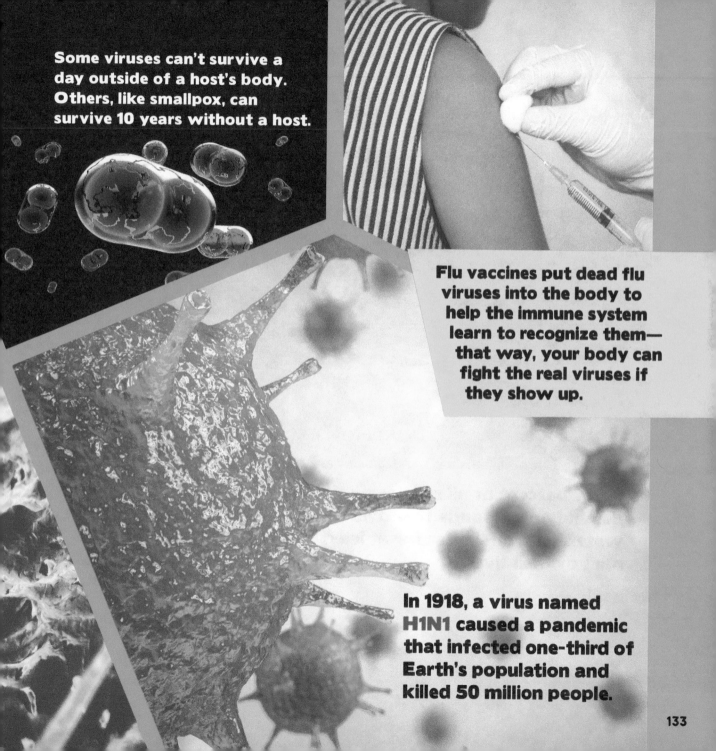

Some viruses can't survive a day outside of a host's body. Others, like smallpox, can survive 10 years without a host.

Flu vaccines put dead flu viruses into the body to help the immune system learn to recognize them— that way, your body can fight the real viruses if they show up.

In 1918, a virus named H1N1 caused a pandemic that infected one-third of Earth's population and killed 50 million people.

WILD WETLANDS

WETLANDS are areas of land that are covered with water for at least part of the year.

Forty percent of all species on Earth depend on wetlands to provide food, water, and/or shelter for at least part of their lives.

There are salt marshes in **NEBRASKA** because it was covered by an ocean 100 million years ago.

BEAVERS can create wetlands by damming up streams to flood an area.

Unlike most plants, **SPARTINA GRASS** can live in salt marshes because it can remove the salt from the water and secrete it from its leaves.

VENUS FLYTRAPS eat bugs to get the nutrients that aren't in wetland soil.

METAMORPHIC ROCKS

When intense heat and pressure turns a rock into a different type of rock, the result is **METAMORPHIC ROCK**.

Pure **LIMESTONE** metamorphizes into white **MARBLE**. If the limestone has iron in it, the marble will be pink. Bits of magnesium make marble green.

A large meteorite impact can create metamorphic rocks like **SHOCKED QUARTZ**.

Metamorphic rocks can become other metamorphic rocks. For example, **SHALE** turns into **SLATE**, which turns into **PHYLLITE**, which turns into **SCHIST**, which turns into **GNEISS**.

SHALE

SLATE

PHYLLITE

GNEISS

SCHIST

Some **GNEISS** rocks reach temperatures of 1,800°F (982°C) during the metamorphic process without melting.

WHEN A STAR DIES

Once a star runs out of fuel, it dies. The most massive stars explode to form **SUPERNOVAE**. The largest supernovae become black holes. Smaller supernovae turn into neutron stars. Stars too small to supernova eventually become white dwarves.

Some supernovae can be hundreds of billions of times brighter than the Sun.

A teaspoon of neutron star would weigh 2 trillion pounds (900 billion kg).

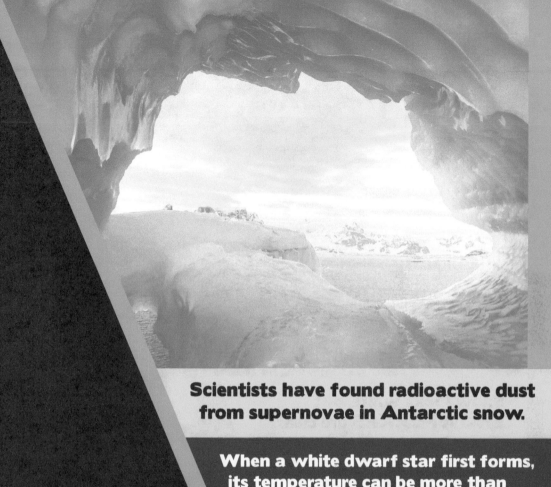

Scientists have found radioactive dust from supernovae in Antarctic snow.

When a white dwarf star first forms, its temperature can be more than 180,000°F (almost 100,000°C). It may take a billion years to cool off.

Not all supernovae are the results of massive stars exploding. White dwarf stars can crash into each other and create a supernova.

THE SKY IS FALLING!

PRECIPITATION is what we call it when water falls from clouds to the ground. Forms of precipitation include rain, sleet, snow, and hail.

Snow looks white, but **SNOWFLAKES** are clear. These ice crystals scatter light in a way that reflects all the colors at the same time, which your eye sees as white.

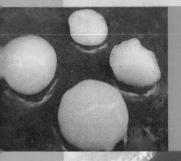

A **HAILSTONE** that fell in South Dakota in 2010 was 8 inches (20 cm) across and weighed almost 2 pounds (0.9 kg)—the size of a pineapple.

CRATER LAKE IS A DEEP LAKE ON TOP OF AN OLD VOLCANO. ALL THE WATER CAME FROM RAIN AND SNOW THAT FELL INTO THE CRATER SINCE ITS ERUPTION 7,700 YEARS AGO.

In 2001, bloodred rain fell in India. The droplets had tiny red particles in them, but scientists are still not sure what they are or where they came from.

FREEZING RAIN falls as a liquid, but when it touches something solid—like a cold tree branch or car windshield—it turns to ice.

141

INCREDIBLE INFRARED

INFRARED WAVES are a kind of radiation. Humans can't see infrared waves, but we can feel them as heat.

A PRISM separates infrared radiation from light. You can't see the infrared rays, but if you put your hand next to the red side, you can feel the heat from them.

The TV remote in your house most likely uses infrared light to tell the TV what to do.

INCOMING SOLAR RADIATION

RERADIATED BACK TO SURFACE

GREENHOUSE GASES

GREENHOUSE GASES trap infrared radiation that rises from the ground after it is heated by the Sun.

MOSQUITOES use infrared light to find animals to bite and to detect the best spots on the body to suck blood.

INFRARED CAMERAS can detect certain kinds of cancer. Tumors give off more heat than the rest of the body, and the infrared camera sees it.

AMAZING ANIMALS OF THE
JURASSIC

The **JURASSIC PERIOD** took place from 201 to 145 million years ago. During this time, the dinosaurs were the largest land animals on Earth.

Apatosaurus had a whip-like tail that could swish fast enough to break the sound barrier and make a small sonic boom.

Castorocauda was a swimming mammal about 20 inches (51 cm) long that looked like a cross between an otter and a beaver.

Epidexipteryx hui was a pigeon-sized dinosaur that had **FEATHERS** to keep it warm and to impress other animals, but it could not fly.

Machimosaurus rex, a prehistoric **CROCODILE**, was more than 30 feet (9 m) long and weighed as much as an elephant.

JURASSIC FLEAS could be almost an inch (21 millimeters) long. They bit dinosaurs like modern fleas bite dogs.

BELOW THE SURFACE

The **MANTLE** is Earth's thickest layer. It is found between the crust and the core.

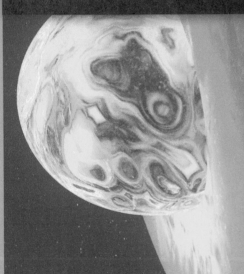

The mantle is almost entirely solid rock, but it can flow like an incredibly slow liquid.

Earth's mantle makes up 84 percent of the planet's volume.

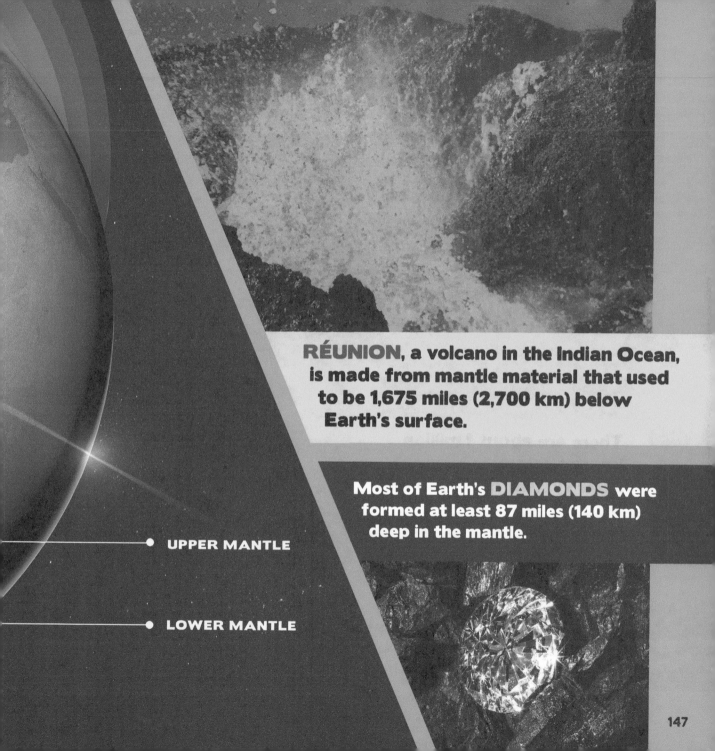

RÉUNION, a volcano in the Indian Ocean, is made from mantle material that used to be 1,675 miles (2,700 km) below Earth's surface.

Most of Earth's **DIAMONDS** were formed at least 87 miles (140 km) deep in the mantle.

UPPER MANTLE

LOWER MANTLE

ROCKS IN SPACE

ASTEROIDS are rocky objects in space that are smaller than planets. Most of the asteroids in our solar system are orbiting the Sun in the asteroid belt.

There are about 1 million known asteroids in our solar system, mostly in the **ASTEROID BELT.**

A large asteroid collision 466 million years ago sent so much dust to Earth that it darkened the skies and started an ice age.

Some of the objects in the asteroid belt, like **HYGIEA** and **CERES**, are large and round enough to be considered dwarf planets.

There is a 1 in 2,700 chance that the skyscraper-sized asteroid **BENNU** will impact with Earth sometime near the end of the 22nd century.

The asteroid that caused dinosaurs and many other species to go extinct created a 112-mile-wide (180 km) impact crater.

SOMETHING FISHY

A **FISH** is a type of animal that lives underwater and has a backbone, fins, and gills.

Fish like the **ARCTIC COD** that live in freezing cold water make their own antifreeze to keep their bodies from turning to ice.

The **ARCHERFISH** can spit a jet of water at a bug to make it fall into the water so the fish can eat it.

GREENLAND SHARKS live longer than any other vertebrate—up to 400 years.

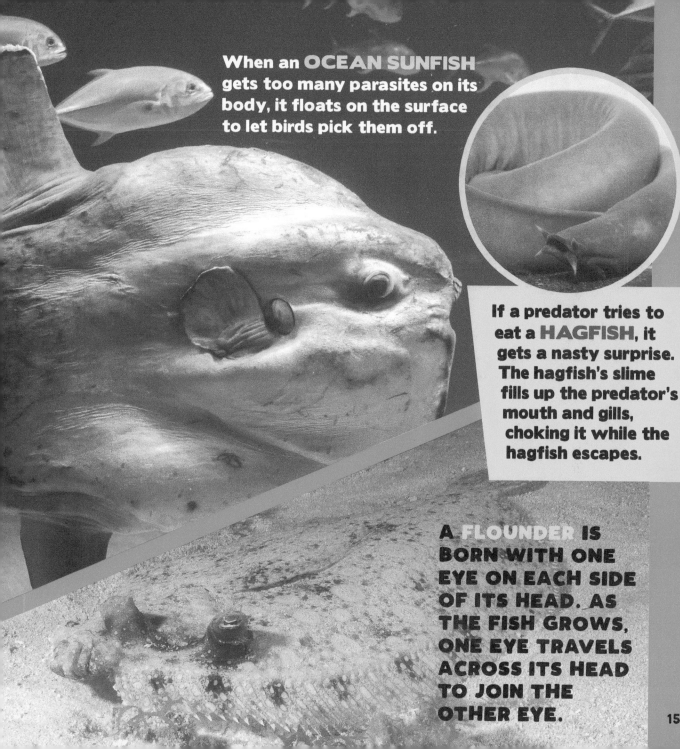

When an **OCEAN SUNFISH** gets too many parasites on its body, it floats on the surface to let birds pick them off.

If a predator tries to eat a **HAGFISH**, it gets a nasty surprise. The hagfish's slime fills up the predator's mouth and gills, choking it while the hagfish escapes.

A **FLOUNDER** IS BORN WITH ONE EYE ON EACH SIDE OF ITS HEAD. AS THE FISH GROWS, ONE EYE TRAVELS ACROSS ITS HEAD TO JOIN THE OTHER EYE.

151

PLASMA APLENTY

PLASMA is the most common state of matter in the universe. It is superheated gas that is electrically charged.

If you raised the temperature of water molecules to 21,630°F (12,000°C), they would become plasma.

Ninety-nine percent of the matter in space is plasma.

The **SUN** sometimes blasts bubbles of plasma across the solar system. The plasma can travel 1 million miles (1.6 million km) per hour through space.

There is plasma on Earth. **LIGHTNING BOLTS**, the neon in glowing signs, and the insides of a plasma **TV** screen are all plasma.

BURNING THE PAST

FOSSIL FUELS like gas, oil, and coal are natural substances made from the remains of living things, which can be burned for energy.

COAL is a sedimentary rock made from the remains of dead plants. Most coal we use today came from trees that lived 300 million years ago.

When a supervolcano called the Siberian Traps ignited nearby coal beds 252 million years ago, the fire released so much carbon dioxide that Earth's climate changed.

In Turkey there is a place where natural gas seeps out of rocks. Called the **FLAMES OF CHIMAERA**, these burning gases have been on fire for thousands of years.

OIL is the remains of ocean plankton and microbes that lived millions of years ago.

Some microbes eat oil and live where oil naturally seeps out of the seafloor.

155

OPPOSITES ATTRACT

A **MAGNET** is an object that produces an invisible magnetic field. Opposite poles of magnets attract each other and like poles repel each other.

Magnets are usually made from **IRON, NICKEL,** and **COBALT**. Gold, silver, copper, lead, and aluminum cannot be magnetized.

The cells of living things are repelled by strong magnets. A **FROG** put on a super-strong magnet will float.

156

MAGLEV TRAINS
USE STRONG MAGNETS THAT REPEL EACH OTHER TO MAKE THE ENTIRE TRAIN HOVER AND MOVE AT SPEEDS UP TO 375 MILES (600 KM) PER HOUR.

The only naturally occurring magnets are called **LODESTONES**. Iron can become a lodestone when it is struck by lightning.

SCIENTISTS HAVE CREATED MAGNETIC LIQUIDS BY PUTTING INCREDIBLY TINY IRON PARTICLES INSIDE THEM.

MINI MERCURY

MERCURY is the rocky planet that is closest to the Sun. It is the smallest planet in the solar system.

Mercury is getting smaller. As it slowly shrinks, it is wrinkling up like a raisin.

Mercury has almost no atmosphere, so it heats up to 800°F (427°C) in the daytime and cools to -290°F (-179°C) at night.

SATURN

NEPTUNE

VENUS

JUPITER

MERCURY

EARTH   MARS

URANUS

Mercury revolves around the Sun in 88 Earth days and rotates once every 59 Earth days. That means a Mercury year lasts 1.3 Mercury days.

Mercury is closest to the Sun, but it is not the hottest planet. VENUS, with its greenhouse gas atmosphere, is hotter.

There's a 1 percent chance that one day the Sun's gravity will knock Mercury out of the solar system, or possibly into another planet.

ADAPTABLE ANIMALS

ADAPTATIONS are behaviors or body parts that help animals, plants, and other living things survive in a particular environment.

AMERICAN DIPPERS are birds that hunt underwater. They have clear eyelids they use like swim goggles to see prey on the river bottom.

LEATHERBACK SEA TURTLES "cry" to remove excess salt from their bodies that they get from eating salty jellyfish.

SLOTHS eat poisonous leaves. They can do this because their stomachs take a month to digest each leaf—giving their livers time to safely remove all the toxins.

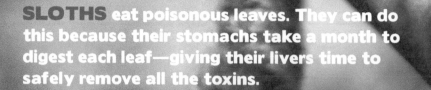

ELEPHANT SEALS dive down more than 2,400 feet (800 m) to find prey. They don't get "the bends," like humans can, because their lungs collapse and blow out all the air.

FLYING SNAKES can jump from tree branches and flatten their bodies to glide—and even turn—through the air.

COOL CARBON

CARBON is an element that is not a metal. It combines with lots of other elements to form new materials called *carbon compounds*.

About 18 percent of your body is made of carbon.

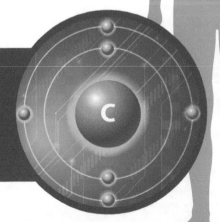

Carbon can combine with so many different atoms that there are about 10 million different molecules that contain carbon.

3,5% — OTHER CHEMICAL ELEMENTS

3,5% — NITROGEN

9,5% — HYDROGEN

18,5% — CARBON

65% — OXYGEN

The two most abundant greenhouse gases, carbon dioxide (CO_2) and methane (CH_4), both contain carbon atoms.

CARBON
DIOXIDE
CO_2

METHANE
CH_4

GRAPHITE and **DIAMONDS** are both made of carbon atoms, but the atoms combine in different ways. Graphite is soft, but diamonds are the hardest substance on Earth.

Carbon atoms can be combined to make **NANOTUBES**, which are 10,000 times thinner than human hairs, but are stronger than steel.

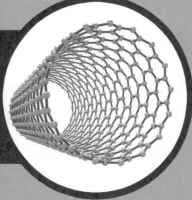

TRENCH VOLCANOES

SUBDUCTION ZONES, also called **TRENCHES**, are places where ocean plates sink under other plates and into the mantle to form volcanoes. Volcanic mountain chains and some islands are formed this way.

The **MAGMA** inside subduction zone volcanoes has a lot of gas that can build up enough pressure to blow lava and ash miles into the sky.

To make a subduction zone volcano, just **ADD WATER**. The water in the seafloor rock lowers the melting temperature of the rock, causing it to melt quickly and rise up.

THE ANTILLES ISLANDS

THE SOUTH SANDWICH ISLANDS

The Pacific Ocean is surrounded by subduction zone volcanoes, but the Atlantic has only two active areas: the ANTILLES ISLANDS and the SOUTH SANDWICH ISLANDS.

Subduction zone volcanoes are near coastlines, so they are often close to large cities. TOKYO and SEATTLE both have volcanoes looming over them.

Subduction zones make island chains where all the islands may be active volcanoes.

PHOTOSYNTHESIS POWERHOUSES

ALGAE are living things that are similar to plants. Like plants, algae make food using photosynthesis. Most seaweeds are algae.

The **GIANT KELP** in kelp forests can be more 100 feet (30 m) tall—as tall as trees.

SPOTTED SALAMANDERS have mutual symbiotic relationships with algae. Their eggs get oxygen from algae while the eggs' waste fertilizes the algae.

166

SARGASSUM lives in the middle of the ocean. It grows little air-filled "balloons" that make it float on the surface so it can carry out photosynthesis.

SEA LETTUCE, a type of seaweed, grows in super-thin sheets that are only one cell thick.

ALGAE grows 10 times faster than land crops and needs much less water, so it may solve hunger and food shortage problems in the future.

SUN-POWERED SOLAR WEATHER

The surface of the Sun blasts particles and plasma into space to create **SOLAR WEATHER**. Solar wind, solar flares, and coronal mass ejections are all types of solar weather.

Earth's magnetic field blocks most solar weather. The aurora borealis, or northern lights, appear when some plasma gets past Earth's protective shield.

Sometimes solar weather can damage communication satellites that our phones use, and it can even disrupt electrical power grids on Earth's surface.

A comet is just a "DIRTY SNOWBALL" until it passes through the Sun's solar wind. Solar wind blasts off bits of the comet and creates the glowing tail we can see from Earth.

Scientists hope to one day attach a 5,200-mile-wide (8,369 km) sail to a satellite that will collect energy from solar wind.

SPINELESS WONDERS

INVERTEBRATES are animals that do not have a spine or backbone. Most of the animals on Earth are invertebrates.

The world's largest invertebrate, the **COLOSSAL SQUID**, has eyes the size of basketballs.

A species of **SHIPWORM** eats stone and poops out sand.

Some small ocean invertebrates, like **SALPS**, use nets made of mucus to catch their prey.

SLUGS are male and female at the same time. They can fertilize their own eggs!

If necessary, a **SCORPION** can slow down its body processes enough to survive while eating only one insect a year.

EXTREME STORMS!

TORNADOES are columns of air that spin up to 300 miles (480 km) per hour. **HURRICANES** are huge, rotating storms that form in the ocean and move to land.

The **UNITED STATES** has the most tornadoes of any country in the world—about 1,250 per year.

The largest tornado ever recorded was 2.6 miles (4.2 km) wide.

A **DOWNBURST** is when wind blows straight down from a thundercloud and spreads in all directions, sometimes at speeds of more than 100 miles (160 km) per hour.

The **EYE** of a hurricane is calm, but the eyewall of the storm that surrounds it has the strongest, most devastating winds.

Storms spin counterclockwise in the Northern Hemisphere and clockwise in the Southern Hemisphere. Storms don't spin at all at the Equator, so hurricanes don't form there.

TWO SENSATIONAL SENSES

TASTE and **SMELL** are senses that animals use to detect what chemical compounds are around them.

Your nose can tell the difference between a trillion different odors, though your brain wouldn't know what to call them all.

When molecules escape from an object, float up your nose, and touch the smell nerve cells, they send a signal to your brain that tells you what you just sniffed.

BUTTERFLIES taste with their feet!

Research shows that ancient predators like *Tyrannosaurus rex* and **SABER-TOOTHED CATS** had powerful senses of smell—just like predators today.

CATS evolved to be meat-eaters, so they can no longer taste sugar.

COMMON MOLES can tell how far away a worm is using only their sense of smell.

175

HOT WATER

GEYSERS and HOT SPRINGS are found in places where magma is close to the surface. Hot springs are places where the water seeps out of the ground gently. Geysers are places where boiling water and steam erupt forcefully out of the ground.

The brilliant green, yellow, orange, and red colors of GRAND PRISMATIC SPRING in Yellowstone are created by bacteria that live in its water.

The tallest geyser in the world is STEAMBOAT GEYSER in Yellowstone. At times, Steamboat can spray hot water 300 feet (90 m) into the air.

MUD POTS smell like rotten eggs because hydrogen sulfide gas is released in the steam that makes the clay bubble.

Even though the **DALLOL HOT SPRINGS** in Ethiopia are extremely hot, salty, and acidic, there are lots of microbes called archaea that live there.

As the amount of magma underground changes, geysers may go extinct. In the 1800s, New Zealand had more than 200 geysers, but now there are about 50.

177

FUNKY FUNGI

FUNGI are living things that are not plants or animals and reproduce with spores. Fungi include mushrooms, mold, and yeast.

When some species of mushrooms are being eaten, they produce **TOXINS** to poison whatever is eating them.

We have millions of microscopic fungi living inside of us that help keep us healthy.

LEAFCUTTER ANTS grow fungus in underground farms to feed to their developing babies.

The biggest organism ever found is a fungus. There is a "**HUMONGOUS FUNGUS**" in Michigan that is mostly underground and covers an area as big as 70 football fields.

Cheese fans love fungus! Many cheeses—like **BRIE, BLUE CHEESE,** and **CAMEMBERT**— get their taste and consistency from the fungi growing on them.

LET THERE BE LIGHT!

VISIBLE LIGHT is a collection of energy waves that we can see. Light includes all the colors.

VISIBLE LIGHT WAVES TRAVEL THROUGH SPACE WITH OTHER WAVES WE CAN'T SEE, LIKE X-RAYS, GAMMA RAYS, RADIO WAVES, INFRARED LIGHT, AND ULTRAVIOLET WAVES.

Scientists have created something called "ULTRA-BLACK" that absorbs all the light that touches it, even laser light.

Moonlight shining through water droplets in the air will create a faint **MOONBOW**.

Red light is weaker than blue light, so it gets blocked by water pretty quickly. This is why red fish in the ocean look black.

Light did not exist until hundreds of thousands, or even millions, of years after the universe formed.

Water scatters light, so the deeper you dive, the more sunlight is blocked. Once you get to 3,280 feet (1000 m) deep, it's pitch-black.

THE COLDEST PLANET

URANUS is the seventh farthest planet from the Sun in our solar system.

Unlike all the other planets, Uranus spins on its axis like a rolling ball instead of like a top.

NEPTUNE

URANUS

Neptune is farthest from the Sun, but Uranus has the coldest temperatures—as cold as -360°F (-218°C).

Uranus has at least 13 rings, but they are so faint that scientists didn't notice them until 1977.

The gravity on Uranus is weaker than Earth's, so you would weigh less there.

The atmosphere of Uranus has some HYDROGEN SULFIDE in it, so this planet would smell like rotten eggs if you visited it.

WATER WORLD

The **OCEAN** is the body of saltwater that covers more than 70 percent of Earth's surface.

The ocean floor is not flat. It has many hills, mountains, plains, and the world's deepest valleys.

The ocean's average depth is 12,080 feet (3,682 m)—more than 2 miles (3.5 km) from the surface to the seafloor!

ASIA

NORTH AMERICA

PACIFIC OCEAN

AUSTRALIA

The Pacific Ocean covers more than 30 percent of the planet. All of the continents would fit inside it.

The ocean is so big that more than 80 percent of it has not been **EXPLORED**. There may be thousands, or even millions, of species there we have not discovered yet.

The **SALT** that is dissolved in ocean water accounts for 3.5 percent of the water's weight.

MICROSCOPIC MICROBES

MICROBES are microscopic living things that consist of only one cell.

YEASTS are single-celled fungi that we use to make bread, beer, and wine.

EUGLENA are microbes that act like plants and animals. They get energy from photosynthesis when the Sun is out but eat things when there is no sunlight.

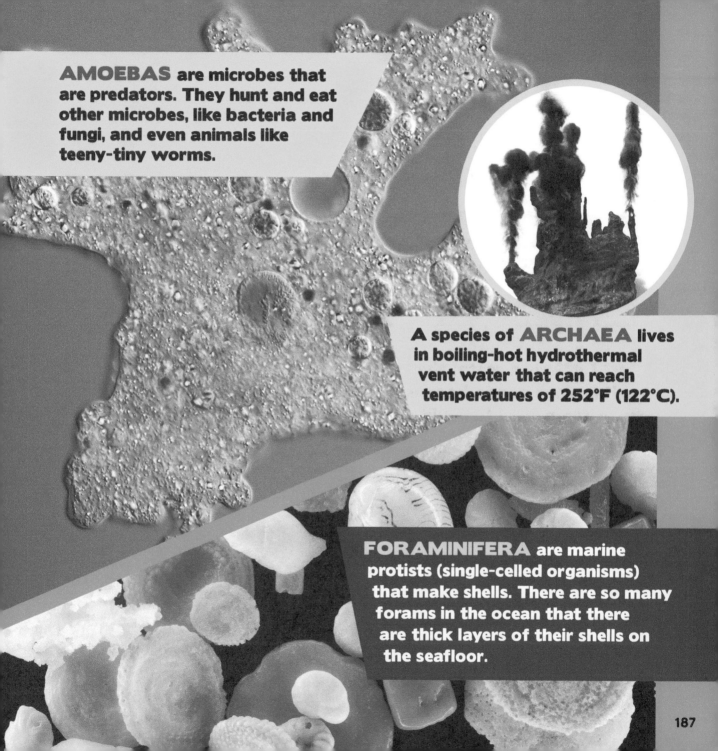

AMOEBAS are microbes that are predators. They hunt and eat other microbes, like bacteria and fungi, and even animals like teeny-tiny worms.

A species of **ARCHAEA** lives in boiling-hot hydrothermal vent water that can reach temperatures of 252°F (122°C).

FORAMINIFERA are marine protists (single-celled organisms) that make shells. There are so many forams in the ocean that there are thick layers of their shells on the seafloor.

SO MANY METALS

METALS are substances that, when solid, tend to be hard, shiny, fairly easy to bend and shape, and good conductors of heat and electricity.

GALLIUM is a metal that will melt in your hands, because it turns from solid to liquid at 86°F (30°C).

ALUMINUM is the most common metal in Earth's crust, but it is hard to find. Many years ago, kings used aluminum to show their wealth.

IRIDIUM is the densest metal, so most of Earth's iridium sank into the core long ago. You can sometimes find iridium on the surface when meteorites bring it here from space.

POTASSIUM is a metal that reacts violently if it contacts water—it explodes!

Mirrors used to be made with **SILVER** because it is the metal that reflects light best.

BRILLIANT BRAINS

The **BRAIN** is an organ found in most (though not all) animals. The brain is like a computer that controls the body and makes decisions.

SEA SQUIRTS have brains when they are babies. When they reach adulthood and stop swimming, most of their brains disappear.

The **GIANT SQUID** has a donut-shaped brain. Its esophagus goes through the donut hole, so everything the squid eats travels through its brain.

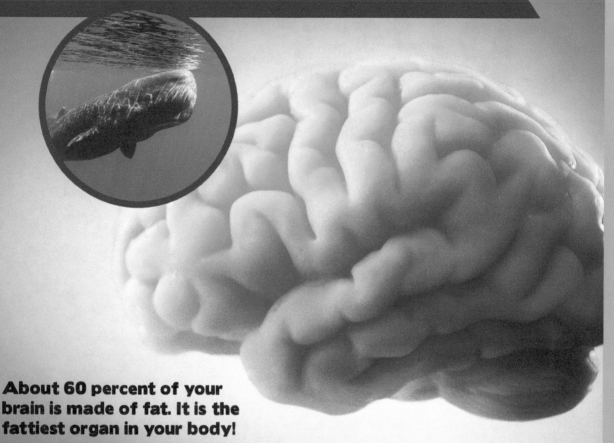

A **SPERM WHALE** weighs about 650 times more than a human, but its brain weighs only 8 times as much as a person's.

About 60 percent of your brain is made of fat. It is the fattiest organ in your body!

Information can travel through your brain at speeds of 268 miles (431 km) per hour—faster than a **NASCAR** car can drive.

EARTH'S CRUST

The **CRUST** is the outer rocky layer of Earth.

Earth's crust makes up only 1 percent of its entire mass. Compared to the rest of Earth, the crust is like the thin skin on an apple.

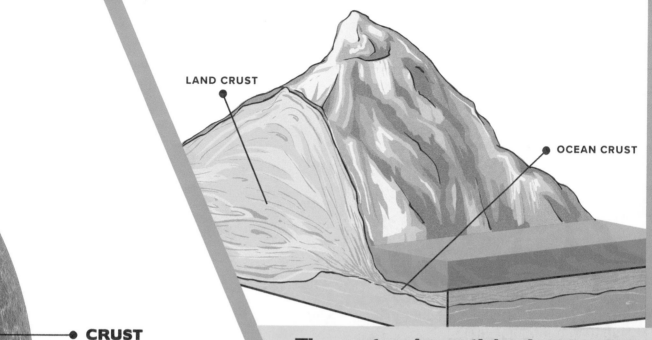

LAND CRUST

OCEAN CRUST

CRUST

The OCEAN CRUST is a lot younger than LAND CRUST. The oldest ocean crust is 270 million years old, but the land crust is more than 4 billion years old.

The crust underneath land averages about 25 miles (40 km) deep. Ocean crust averages about 5 miles (8 km) deep.

Since 1959, scientists have been trying to drill all the way through the crust, but they haven't made it yet. Their deepest attempt was 40,230 feet (12 km).

Even though the Moon is a lot smaller than Earth, its crust is thicker than Earth's—about 38 to 63 miles (60 to 100 km) thick.

AMAZING ANIMALS OF THE
PALEOZOIC SEA

The **PALEOZOIC ERA** took place from 541 to 252 million years ago. Plants and animals first appeared on land then, but the most diverse life was in the ocean.

Armored fish called **PLACODERMS** looked like they had teeth, but the "teeth" were actually bony plates that stuck out of their jaws.

OPABINIA was a little shrimplike predator that had five eyes and a long mouthpart with a claw at the end that it used to grab prey.

Sharks first appeared during the Paleozoic. **EDESTUS SHARKS** had jaws like two jagged scissor blades that they used to slice prey in half.

Some of the 20,000 species of **TRILOBITES** that lived during the Paleozoic could curl into balls to protect themselves.

During part of the Paleozoic, some of the biggest ocean predators were **SEA SCORPIONS**, like the one that left this fossil, that were 8 feet (2.5 m) long.

POTENT POISONS

POISONS are toxic substances that can cause injury or death to a living thing.

Plants that produce nicotine—like **TOBACCO** and **TOMATOES**—use it to poison animals that are trying to eat them.

LEAD is poisonous because it is too much like calcium. Our bodies think the lead is calcium and try to use it the same way, which ends up killing brain and nerve cells.

BLUE-CAPPED IFRITS are birds that eat poisonous beetles. The beetles' poison makes its way into the birds' feathers, making them poisonous too.

CYANIDE can be a deadly poison and yet you might eat it every day. Peaches, spinach, corn, and sweet potatoes all have tiny amounts of cyanide—not nearly enough to hurt you.

Things can become poisonous when you take too much of them. Even **WATER** can be a poison if you drink it in huge amounts.

197

INCREDIBLE INSECTS

INSECTS are invertebrate animals that have six legs and three-part bodies.

CUCKOO WASPS lay their eggs in other wasp species' nests. The cuckoo wasps hatch and eat the other wasp babies in the nest.

During a single year, one LADYBUG may eat 5,000 other bugs.

TERMITE QUEENS in Africa lay an egg every three seconds for as long as 15 years straight.

PRAYING MANTISES are amazing predators. Some have even snatched and eaten hummingbirds, mice, and lizards!

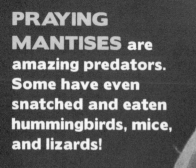

BULLET ANTS have a sting that is so intensely painful, it feels like you've been shot—and the pain lasts for up to 24 hours!

The **SEA SKATER** walks on ocean water. If a wave knocks it underwater, air bubbles on the skater's leg hairs make it float back to the surface.

WHAT DON'T WE KNOW?

Science is not just a list of facts. It is a way of learning new things. There are many things we still don't know about our bodies, our planet, and our universe.

We don't know what makes up about 70 percent of the universe. So far, almost all of the universe is completely invisible to us.

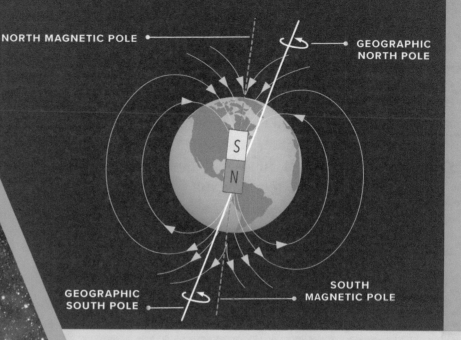

NORTH MAGNETIC POLE

GEOGRAPHIC NORTH POLE

S

N

GEOGRAPHIC SOUTH POLE

SOUTH MAGNETIC POLE

We aren't sure what causes Earth's magnetic poles to regularly switch back and forth from north to south.

We don't know how many species are living today. Scientists think that as many as 90 percent of species on Earth have not been discovered and named yet.

We aren't sure why we dream—or even why we and other animals need to sleep.

We know that the trillions of microbes living in our bodies help us, but we still don't how most of them help or what most of them are doing.

Kevin Kurtz is an award-winning children's author who specializes in nonfiction books about science and nature. He has been lucky enough to work with scientists studying ocean animals, volcanoes, and the asteroid impact that caused the extinction of the dinosaurs. Kevin lives in Rochester, New York, where he continues to write books and do programs with schools to introduce kids to the wonders all around us. Learn more about him at KevKurtz.com.

NOTES

NOTES

NOTES

NOTES

NOTES

NOTES

NOTES

NOTES

NOTES